PROJECT ESTIMATING AND COST MANAGEMENT

The books in the Project Management Essential Library series provide project managers with new skills and innovative approaches to the fundamentals of effectively managing projects.

Additional titles in the series include:

Managing Projects for Value, John C. Goodpasture

Effective Work Breakdown Structures, Gregory T. Haugan

Project Planning and Scheduling, Gregory T. Haugan

Managing Project Quality, Timothy J. Kloppenborg and Joseph A. Petrick

Project Measurement, Steve Neuendorf

Project Risk Management: A Proactive Approach, Paul S. Royer

MANAGEMENTCONCEPTS

www.managementconcepts.com

PROJECT ESTIMATING AND COST MANAGEMENT

Parviz F. Rad

𝔪

MANAGEMENTCONCEPTS

Vienna, Virginia

⟪⟪
MANAGEMENTCONCEPTS

8230 Leesburg Pike, Suite 800
Vienna, VA 22182
(703) 790-9595
Fax: (703) 790-1371
www.managementconcepts.com

Printed in the United States of America

Library of Congress Cataloging-in-Publication Data

Rad, Parviz F., 1942–
    Project estimating and cost management/Parviz F. Rad.
       p. cm. — (Project management essential library)
    Includes bibliographical references and index.
    ISBN 978-1-56726-144-8 (pbk.)
    ISBN 1-56726-144-2
    1. Cost control. I. Title. II. Series.
TS167.R43 2001
658.15'52—dc21

                                              2001049446

About the Author

Parviz F. Rad holds an M.Sc. from Ohio State University and a Ph.D. from the Massachusetts Institute of Technology. He has more than 30 years of professional experience, during which he has served in governmental, industrial, and academic capacities. He has participated in project management activities and in the development and enhancement of quantitative tools in project management in a multitude of disciplines, including software development, construction, and pharmaceutical research. Dr. Rad is a professional civil engineer, a certified cost engineer, and a project management professional.

I Dedicate This Book
to the Memory of My Parents

Table of Contents

Preface xi
Acknowledgments xiii

CHAPTER **1**   **Introduction** 1
    Project Scope and Objectives 2
    Organizational Objectives 5
    Project Selection 6

CHAPTER **2**   **Deliverable-Oriented Work**
                Breakdown Structure 11
    Work Breakdown Structure 12
    WBS Development Steps 13
    The Division Bases 13
    Case Example: WBS for an Industrial Complex 15
    Comparison of the Different Bases 16
    Process-Oriented Projects 17
    Organizational Priorities 19
    Semantics 21
    Changing the Paradigm 22

CHAPTER **3**   **Resource Breakdown Structure** 27
    Nomenclature, Dimensions, and Units 28
    Resource Breakdown Structure 29
    RBS Development 31
    The Primary Division Basis 32
    Lower-Level Division Bases with a Concentration
       on Human Resources 34
    Estimating the Costs 36
    Detailed Example 38

CHAPTER **4**   **Estimating Models** 43
    Accuracy 47

Parametric Estimating 50
   Modular Estimating 50
   Parametric Model 51
Analogous Estimating 53
   Ratio Estimating 54
   The Three-Quarters Rule 55
   The Square Root Rule 59
   The Two-Thirds Rule 61
Range Estimating 62
Expert Judgment 64
Normalization 64

CHAPTER 5 **Progress Monitoring** 67
Developing a Monitoring Plan 70
Elements of Monitoring 73
Earned Value 75
Productivity 78

CHAPTER 6 **Cost Management** 81
Causes of Change 85
Feed-Forward Technique 87
Impact of Schedule on Cost 88
Lifecycle Costs 94
Impact of Project Risk 95

CHAPTER 7 **External Projects** 99
Specifications 100
Contracts 102
Response to Specifications 106
Bidding 108
Project Costs 110
   Direct Costs 110
   Indirect Costs 110
   Overhead 111
   Allowance 111
   Contingency 112
Project Audit 112

Bibliography 115
Index 117

Preface

Many of the currently available books on estimating cover project estimating in a discipline-specific mode, such as construction estimating, software development estimating, and process plant estimating. Although there is a great deal of commonality in estimating techniques among all industries, distilling the nondiscipline-specific topics is sometimes difficult because they tend to get masked by the details of the discipline that is the subject of the project.

Project Estimating and Cost Management covers the fundamentals of estimating projects in a discipline-independent context. It covers the essentials of project estimating, progress monitoring, and cost management, and is intended for project professionals who need a quick overview of the process of estimating the cost of projects. Special attention is focused on estimate accuracy and the issues surrounding cost and schedule overruns.

Chapter 1 deals with the inception of the project as it relates to organizational strategies. Project selection and prioritization using indices and models are also presented. Chapters 2 and 3 describe the development of work breakdown structures (WBS) and resource breakdown structures (RBS), with detailed discussions of the elements and bases of division for these structures. These chapters guide the reader through the steps involved in constructing WBS and RBS. The reader is then introduced to the concept of bottom-up estimating and the steps involved in creating a detailed estimate baseline.

Chapter 4 discusses the various models that estimators use to arrive at rough estimates of projects during the early stages of project conception. The issues of estimate accuracy and baseline volatility are discussed, recognizing both the need to provide estimates in order to make judgments on project authorization and the scarcity of detailed data (at the time these estimates are developed).

Chapters 5 and 6 focus on the processes and techniques involved in monitoring project expenditures during the implementation phase. Data collected by the monitoring activities will form the knowledge base that the project manager will need to deal with the inevitable changes that occur during project implementation. The causes of these changes to the project environment and the procedures involved in formulating resolutions for these unexpected changes are also discussed.

Chapter 7 deals with estimating and cost management issues related to external projects. The topics of bidding, specifications, indirect costs, and overhead are discussed, specifically relating to contractor performance and its impact on the client-contractor relationship.

Parviz F. Rad

Acknowledgments

The author would like to thank *Dr. Denis F. Cioffi* for co-authoring Chapter 3 of this book. The author would also like to thank *Mr. Vittal Anantalmula* for reviewing the book and providing many helpful suggestions.

CHAPTER 1

Introduction

Estimating is the art and science of using historical data, personal expertise, institutional memory, and the project scope statement to predict the resource expenditures, total cost, and duration of a project. A typical statement of project objectives will outline the attributes of a new physical deliverable, the details of performance enhancements to a system, or the purpose of a specific service. To estimate the project cost, the project manager must identify the various constituent physical elements and related activities necessary to meet the project objectives. Next, the project manager develops the estimate by summing the estimate of resources for these elements. Then, by extension, the project manager computes the elemental and project costs.

When the project is conceived, the estimate is extremely inaccurate because very little information is available about the expected deliverables, the project team, and the project environment. But, as the project evolves and more information becomes available, the estimate can be fine-tuned to a higher level of precision. Details of the objective, scope, quality, and desired delivery date are necessary for a comprehensive and accurate estimate. As these details become available, they in turn trigger enhancements in the work breakdown structure (WBS), the estimate, the schedule, and other planning documents. Further, the evolving planning documents could also include increasing details about the procedures that will be used in implementing the project.

The initial cost estimates of the elements and the project form the baseline budget for measuring the cost performance of the project during the implementation phase. This cost estimate, and therefore the budget, are initially very rough and inaccurate. When establishing the project budget on the basis of the project estimate, it is necessary to note whether the estimate was developed using a rough conceptual estimate technique or a detailed bottom-up estimate. If the budget was established during the early stages of project planning, the budget development process should allow some modification flexibility, primarily because early estimates are inaccurate.

Likewise, during the implementation phase, the project estimate serves as the base of reference for developing quantitative indicators of the project cost performance. Accordingly, depending on the accuracy and limitations of the estimate, appropriate contingencies, reserves, and flexibilities should also be incorporated into the budget. It is important to remember the degree of accuracy of the baseline estimate when making commitments, comparisons, and judgments during the budget development and project progress monitoring phases. In progressive organizations, the amount of budgeted funds for the project will go through several modifications as the details develop.

The credibility, accuracy, and completeness of the estimate are enhanced by the estimator's skills in the areas of business, finance, engineering, technology, information systems, manufacturing, assembly, marketing, management, production planning, and all facets of project management activities. Since it is somewhat unrealistic to expect one person to have expertise in all these areas, organizations sometimes form estimating committees or estimating boards. The board members contribute their expertise from all technical disciplines impacted by the project such as business development, purchasing, contracting, financial management, and of course, project management.

The project's cost estimate is derived by summing the resource expenditures and, consequently, the cost of the project's individual component parts of the WBS. Likewise, with the hopeful expectation that estimating and scheduling processes use the same WBS, the estimate of the duration of the project's component WBS elements is used in the development of the schedule network, which in turn formulates a time management structure. Therefore, there is an interdependent relationship between the project's cost and the schedule. This interdependence must be taken into account during project implementation, when the changes in scope and specifications cause changes in the project's cost and/or schedule. Furthermore, this relationship between cost and schedule must be continually reviewed as the project matures, detailed project plans are formulated, more definitive baselines are established, and finally, the inevitable tradeoffs are made during the implementation phase.

PROJECT SCOPE AND OBJECTIVES

The client's needs and desires are communicated to the project personnel through documents such as the project's charter, objectives, scope statement, and specifications. The terms *requirements specifications* and *scope* have been used interchangeably and sometimes differently depending on the industry in which the project is being implemented. Construction, industrial, and process projects refer to the description of the deliverable as *scope* and *specifications*. *Scope* refers to a broader expression of the client's objectives while the term *specifications* refers to the detailed expression of the client's objectives. Systems and software development projects often do not use the term *scope* while referring to deliverables, but they use the term *requirements* to describe the performance attributes of the projects, such as processing speed, error rate, database size, and the degree of friendliness of the deliverables. Systems and software projects use the term *specifications* to describe the attributes of the hardware. Hardware specifications for systems and software development projects might be either predetermined by the client as part of the project objectives or developed by the project team as one of the deliverable components.

Sometimes the quality of the project deliverable is not explicitly addressed as part of the definition of project objectives. Ironically, it is this issue of quality—independent of the volume of deliverables—that determines the usability of the product and the resulting satisfaction of the stakeholders. For the purposes of this book, quality and scope are treated collectively.

Project specifications are usually included in the contract documents if the project is an external project, and particularly if the contract is awarded on a lump sum basis. However, enlightened organizations develop specifications documents even for their internal projects. The objectives or specifications of an internal project are usually spelled out in the authorization memo that empowers the project manager to implement the project. The rationale for using specifications for an internal project is that, although an internal project does not involve a contract, it should have a set of well-defined scope and objectives, so that the delivery performance can be carefully monitored. The premise is that evaluation and monitoring of internal projects will become an ad-hoc activity if there are no focused objectives and, therefore, no detailed specifications.

The *scope document* includes the client's wants and needs, the distinction being that "wants" are those items that would be desirable to have although not crucial to the success of the project, while "needs" are those items that are essential to the success and usability of the project deliverable. Again, this information will probably be very sketchy during the early stages of project evolution, and will be refined, clarified, and progressively elaborated as more information becomes available to the client and the project team.

Definition of project objectives involves detailing the project scope, attributes of the deliverables, acceptance tests, desired delivery date, expected budget, and team structure. When the client directs the activities of the project, the description of tools and techniques used in implementing the project are also included in the specifications document.

To some extent, the acceptance procedures and validation tests determine the physical quality and performance tolerances of the deliverable. Therefore, care should be taken to ensure that the tests reflect all the important operational facets of the product, and that these tests do not reflect frivolous features. In the same vein, the team should make every effort to craft the deliverable to the spirit of these tests and not necessarily to the letter of the tests, which might miss some important facet of the product. Due diligence on the part of the project team will promote client satisfaction, which is considered one of the most important indicators of a project's success.

The *desired delivery date* signifies the date on which the client wishes to begin reaping the benefits of the deliverables, and, therefore, the most important date for the project's schedule. Notwithstanding, for a variety of historical and operational reasons, several intermediate milestones are usually defined as part of project plans. Intermediate milestones are not crucial to the execution of the project, but the achievement of these milestones often signifies or verifies the expected pace of the project and the desired quality of the deliverables. The establishment of intermediate milestones can be in response to the needs and desires of the client, the collective project team, individual team members, or the stakeholders.

A carefully drafted project objective document is essential to the project's success. The *objective statement* is the focal point and the definitive reference source for managing the triple constraints of the project during the implementation phase. Project procedures must include instructions on how to treat the project objective statement as a living document to be enhanced continually, albeit the current version of this statement will be used as a base of performance reference through the life of the project. Project management procedures must highlight uniform and consistent guidelines for the development of, and making modifications to, the baseline project objectives and specifications.

Project planning documents must include details of processes, procedures, and methodologies that will be used for monitoring the effectiveness and efficiency of the project team in implementing the project deliverable. Since the characteristics of the team can have subtle but significant impact on the project's success, the characteristics of the project team must be outlined in planning the physical deliverable of the project. Team attributes that must be addressed are the skill of team members, the administrative affiliation of team members, and the time spent on other duties during the project at hand. Further, project management activities dealing with team formation and team charter must be well defined and planned during the very early stages.

Particularly in external projects, the major items of equipment used to craft the project deliverable and to test its important attributes should be included. For external projects, the number of subcontractors and the overall contracting strategy must be carefully evaluated in the light of the best interests of the project and its business plan, and not just on the basis of the lowest initial cost. Contracting strategy will impact the communication pattern among project stakeholders, and will subtly affect project performance.

The fee structure of a contractor can profoundly affect the total project cost. Therefore, a careful analysis of direct costs, indirect costs, overhead, and the contractor's profit margin is advisable, particularly if the contract is being awarded on a cost-plus basis.

A review of marginal or failed projects shows that the vast majority suffered from lack of detailed planning, or casual and ad-hoc procedures for managing the project's changes. Conversely, the literature shows that organizations that encourage detailed planning of projects experience far better financial growth when compared to organizations that do not. Finally, data support the concept that organizations that employ competent project management professionals and consistent project management procedures tend to produce more successful projects.[1,2]

ORGANIZATIONAL OBJECTIVES

Projects are usually undertaken in response to a set of goals that is identified to achieve organizational objectives. The most common categories of organizational objectives include operating necessity, competitive necessity, or innovative ventures. Therefore, as a prelude to project selection and initiation, organizational priorities must be clearly identified and clarified.

One of the important components of a project definition document is the rationale statement detailing how the project investment is reconciled with organizational strategic goals and investment policies. Further, with innovative and creative crafting of project objectives, it is possible for a project management team to develop alternative options in achieving the same organizational goal. Finally, a project should be considered for authorization after considering individuals' current workloads, the divisions' operational obligations, and the parent organization's current financial obligations.

The planning documents for each project must include all available data on the project's sponsor, objectives, and deadline. The project's business plan must clearly articulate the reasons for initiating this project and the expected benefits of the project's deliverable. Further, in many ways, implicit or explicit corporate support for the project determines the organizational viability and the project's importance. A signal that there is insufficient administrative support for the project is that senior management is not willing to sponsor it. To satisfy this requirement, key executives and major stakeholders sponsoring the project must be identified in project charter documents.

To reconcile the project costs with the corporate investment strategies, each project must have a business objective, which serves as the foundation for the project's investment proposal. The document containing the project objectives and investment strategies is called a *business case* or a *business plan*. The business plan should provide ample information on the project deliverable's utility, which will then be used to determine whether or not the project should be funded for implementation. It also should provide details of all costs, benefits, and risks associated with the delivery of the proposed project.

To meet this mandate, the business plan must provide a detailed description of the problem, need, or opportunity to which the project is expected to respond. Then, the alternative projects that respond to the same opportunity must be highlighted in terms of expected deliverables, conceptual estimate, preliminary schedule, and a quantified list of benefits and risks.

The business plan for a specific organizational objective may be related to several alternative projects. These projects offer slightly different deliverables and yet they all would achieve the same general business objectives. In some cases, one project might impact two separate organizational strategies. Therefore, in a proactive and dynamic organization, it is normal to have a large portfolio of possible projects. However, funding limitations usually preclude implementation of all these projects. Consequently, a formalized project ranking and selection process must be developed to identify the projects with the most impact on the organizational needs at hand, at the lowest possible funding, and with optimized values of other issues important to the organization.

PROJECT SELECTION

Selection of projects for implementation must be performed in consideration of the organization's needs and wants, corporate strategic plans, realistic expectations for sophistication of the deliverables, success attributes of the project, and the constraints for the project's success. To make consistent and logical decisions in prioritizing and selecting projects, a company-specific process of evaluating projects must be established.

Ranking of projects is most commonly conducted with the use of an index, sometimes called a metric, or a group of indices called a *model*. In general, models are easy-to-use characterizations of operations, organizations, and relationships. The models range from very simple to very complex, although all models, even the very sophisticated ones, are only a partial representation of the reality that they attempt to portray.

Although models are very useful as aids in the decision-making process, they do not fully duplicate all facets of the real world. On the other hand, with this focused feature of models in mind, models can be exploited to purge extraneous elements of a problem and to highlight the important elements of the issues surrounding project implementation. The objective of the project selection process is to rank the projects for implementation in the organization's best interest. The selection process, therefore, would use a model that is specifically formulated to optimize parameters such as organizational goals, project cost, project duration, and the anticipated attributes of the project deliverable.

The numeric results of the model must always be tempered by the experience and professional expertise of the organizational entity charged with managing the project portfolio. Ideally, this entity is the project management office, although the function might be performed by an ad-hoc, or standing, team designated by upper management. The project portfolio management group is expected to make a judgment on project viability using information generated by the model, and in consideration of the model's limitations and constraints and/or its constituent indices. This judgment, however, will be partly predicated on the quantified rankings provided by the models or indices.

During a typical project selection process, it is necessary to identify organizational priorities for projects, establish metrics to evaluate project objectives in the light of these priorities, and formulate company-specific scoring schemas for the project ranking process. There are four sets of basic elements for the selection process: organizational priorities, project objectives, the selection model, and the ranking process (see Figure 1-1).

Indices used for project selection tend to fall into two major categories. The first category includes quantitative indices that are generally based on financial characteristics such as:
- Total cost
- Cash flow demand

FIGURE 1-1 Project Selection

Project Objectives   Organizational Priorities

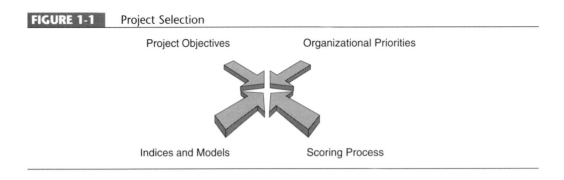

Indices and Models   Scoring Process

- Cost-benefit ratio
- Payback period
- Average internal rate of return
- Net present value.

The second category includes qualitative indices that are intended to measure subjective issues, such as operational necessity, competitive necessity, product line extension, market constraints, desirability, recognition, and success (see Figure 1-2).

A project selection model is very organization-specific and should use a customized combination of indices to satisfy the organizational project selection objectives. Since models depend on numeric input from the indices, even subjective indices ultimately will have to be quantified. Accordingly, a measure of refinement will be added to the selection process if the quantification of the subjective model indices is based on consistent and organization-specific procedures. Then, using the project data, organizational priorities,

FIGURE 1-2 Qualitative Indices

- Organizational Support
- Value to the Customer
- Value to the Shareholders
- Public Recognition
- Internal Recognition
- Employee Education
- Customer Education
- Innovation
- Information Retention

- Workload Demand
- High-Level Support
- Operational Necessity
- Competitive Necessity
- Product Line Extension
- Feasibility
- On-Time Probability
- On-Budget Probability
- Marketing Considerations
- Profitability

customized model, and a consistent scoring process, it is possible to systematically, and in a formalized fashion, rank the prospective projects.

Figure 1-3 shows a graphical depiction of a selection model that is composed of four indices. The simple summation or weighted summation of the results of the indices is used to compute the rating of the project by this model. Figure 1-4 shows a sample of a customized model. The possible total points for a project are 100 and, therefore, prospective projects can be compared on the basis of the total score yielded by this model. The importance of each of the indices in this model is signified by the points assigned to each index, which has been customized for a particular organization. The relative importance of these indices is reflected by how many maximum possible points are assigned to each index.

To extend the illustration a bit further, a hypothetical project might receive a total score of 60 points on the basis of the scoring that the project received on individual indices that were identified and ranked specifically for that organization (see Figure 1-5). It should be noted that the score of an individual project is not as important as the relative scores of several projects that were ranked using the same model and the same rating process.

When conducting project comparisons, it is useful and logical to normalize the base of reference. One of the more convenient techniques is to

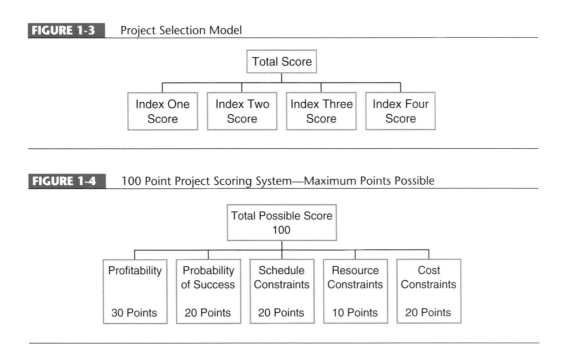

FIGURE 1-3   Project Selection Model

FIGURE 1-4   100 Point Project Scoring System—Maximum Points Possible

FIGURE 1-5   100 Point Project Scording System—Total Project Score

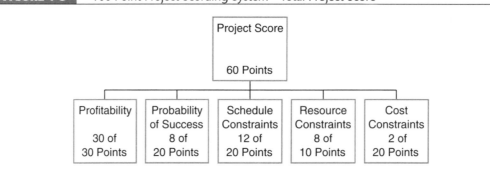

use the direct cost as the base of reference for the prospective projects. Compartmentalizing the direct cost of the project from other elements has the advantage of developing a project estimate strictly from the standpoint of the level of effort. Other elements such as indirect costs, overhead, and return on investment are important values; however, since they tend to be somewhat variable with organizational entity and time, they might add unnecessary inaccuracy to the project selection process.

Estimating is a very inexact science during the early periods of a project's life. Ironically, the very early estimates of a project become one of the critical factors in determining whether the project reaches the next stage by virtue of allocation of funds. Naturally, the accuracy of any given estimate is enhanced by a detailed and focused set of project objectives. Organizational objectives and deliverable expectations also play important roles in selecting a project for implementation. A formalized project selection procedure will include a selection model consisting of several quantified indices that reflect the project attributes in the light of the organizational priorities and objectives.

NOTES

1. C.W. Ibbs and Y.H. Kwak, *The Benefits of Project Management—Financial and Organizational Rewards to Corporations* (Sylva, NC: PMI® Publications, 1997).
2. M.R.Vigder and A.W. Kark, *Software Cost Estimation and Control* (Ottawa, Ontario, Canada: National Research Council of Canada, February 1994).

CHAPTER 2

Deliverable-Oriented Work Breakdown Structure

A work breakdown structure (WBS) provides a framework of common reference for all project elements, specific tasks within the project, and ultimately better schedules and better estimates. A WBS facilitates the integration of project plans for time, resources, and quality. An effective WBS encourages a systematic planning process, reduces the possibility of omission of key project elements, and simplifies the project by dividing it into manageable units. If the WBS is used as the common skeleton for the schedule and the estimate, it facilitates communication among the professionals implementing the project.

Before addressing the WBS, it is useful to set the proper perspective for project structures. Three separate structures need to be created, defined, or modified for the purposes of a project: (1) the organizational breakdown structure (OBS), (2) the resource breakdown structure (RBS), and (3) the WBS.

The OBS is the most readily available structure. Since companies frequently go through massive organizational changes, it is necessary to use the most current data with frequent updates as changes occur to the reporting lines of the organization. For the purposes of the project management system, the organizational chart must be augmented by unwritten responsibilities and by dotted-line relationships that affect the execution of the project.

The RBS is a logical and useful classification of the resources necessary to accomplish the project objectives. Rather than developing a new RBS for each project, it is more efficient to develop an RBS for a large family of projects. As each new project is planned, only those portions of this common

This chapter is an adaptation of a paper authored by Parviz F. Rad as published in Volume 41, No, 12, pp. 35-39 of *Cost Engineering* and titled *Advocating a Deliverable-Oriented Work Breakdown Structure.* Reprinted with the permission of AACE International, 209 Prairie Ave., Suite 100, Morgantown, WV 25601 USA. Phone: 800-858-COST/304-296-8444. Fax: 304-291-5728. Internet: http://www.aacei.org. E-mail: info@aacei.org.

RBS that apply to the project will be selected and used. A project RBS is different from all other human resource or budgeting classification methods in that it reflects applicability to project management as compared to cost accounting or to personnel evaluations. An RBS is essentially a catalog of all the resources that are available to the project. RBS development will be discussed in Chapter 3.

The most difficult to define, and yet the most useful of these three project structures, is the WBS. Its information is drawn primarily from the project objectives statement, historical files of past projects, project performance reports, or any other files containing the original and final project objectives of previous projects. As with the RBS, sometimes it is appropriate to develop a general WBS for a family of projects, and then for each project only the appropriate segments need to be selected and modified. This practice is appropriate in organizations that conduct projects that are somewhat similar albeit not identical.

WORK BREAKDOWN STRUCTURE

As defined previously, the WBS is a uniform, consistent, and logical method for dividing the project into small, manageable components for purposes of planning, estimating, and monitoring. A deliverable-oriented WBS facilitates and encourages the feed-forward of information within the project. Ideally, it is uniform and consistent. To achieve uniformity, all parts of the WBS must be developed using the same criteria. The ultimate goal is to achieve a WBS that will highlight a logical organization of products, parts, and modules.

A WBS will provide a roadmap for planning, monitoring, and managing all facets of the project, such as the following:

- Definition of work
- Cost estimates
- Budgeting
- Time estimates
- Scheduling
- Resource allocation
- Expenditures
- Changes to the project plan
- Productivity
- Performance.

As the project is conceived, defined, and fully developed, not only summaries for the WBS can be created for one project, but also departmental and divisional summaries can be made for each WBS item. These summaries use the relationship between the RBS and the WBS and are quite useful for resource forecasting, personnel projections, priority definitions, and general management purposes.

WBS DEVELOPMENT STEPS

Simply stated, development of a WBS involves grouping all project elements into several (between three and nine) categories, called *level one* (see Figure 2-1). Each level one item will be divided into three to nine *level two* items, each of the level two items will be divided into three to nine *level three* items, and so on. It is crucial that, at each juncture, the basis of division be the same for all parts of the project.

Ideally, a reasonable consistency is maintained in the degree of detail at the lowest level elements. Not all branches need to go to the same level, but the significance of all of the lowest level items in the overall project should be similar. Therefore, depending on the project, some branches may go to level two, some to level three, and some even to level five.

This process is continued until the project has been divided into manageable, discrete, and identifiable items requiring simple tasks to complete. *A rule of thumb*: Keep dividing the project until the elements cannot be divided realistically. This point varies from company to company and among project managers within the same company. The contents of each level of detail are not only company-specific, but they are also specific to the nature of deliverables involved in each project. The degree of detail at the lowest level of each branch must be in line with the size of the project and in conformance with the company's operational philosophies.

THE DIVISION BASES

To put things in the proper perspective, the transition from each level of WBS to the next level may be on any one of the following bases:

- *Deliverable-Oriented*
  —Product
  —Functional system
  —Physical area

FIGURE 2-1   Work Breakdown Structure

- Divide the Work into 3 to 9 Categories
- Divide Each Category into 3 to 9 Packages
- Divide Each Package into 3 to 9 Modules
- Divide........
- Divide........
- Divide........

- *Schedule-Oriented*
  —Task or activity
  —Sequential
- *Resource-Oriented*
  —Discipline
  —Administrative unit
  —Budget account.

There is some overlap in definition and usage between the items of a subgroup of these eight bases, i.e., between product, functional system, and physical location. It is possible for one person to divide the project on the basis of product and, depending on the nature of the project, someone else might view the division as having been on the basis of physical location.

The *product basis* refers to those cases where the project is divided into individual distinct components that ultimately comprise the project, such as hardware, software, physical structure, south wall, north wall, concrete foundation, or steel roof. The *functional basis* refers to the functional systems that provide a particular facet of the infrastructure for the project deliverable. Functional systems are usually interwoven into the product. Examples of functional systems include the electrical system, the mechanical system, or the skeleton of a building. The *physical area basis* highlights the geographical or physical locations of the deliverable (e.g., south side, north side, top floor, entrance). It is important to note that the most useful, and admittedly the most difficult, procedure for developing a WBS is to use the deliverable as the basis of breakdown of the project.

Task or *activity basis* refers to things that project team members do toward the goals of the project, such as excavating, pouring, forming, polishing, programming, testing, etc. *Sequential basis* reflects the order in which activities are performed, such as Phase I, Phase II, Phase III, etc. The sequence is often dictated by administrative constraints and may be somewhat arbitrary. Use of these two bases is akin to importing the project schedule into the WBS. Ideally, the WBS should be used to develop the schedule—and not the other way around.

The *administrative unit basis* is an infusion of the OBS elements into the WBS and indicates the administrative or organizational division lines. Examples include work done by employees of division A, division B, or the contract office. The *budget account basis* is an infusion of the RBS into the WBS and will follow the organization's financial structure, such as activities paid by federal funds, state funds, charge account A, or fiscal account B. Here again, the WBS should be used to develop the costs and resource assignments, and funding procedures should not influence the nature of the project.

CASE EXAMPLE: WBS FOR AN INDUSTRIAL COMPLEX

What follows will give a comparison between the deliverable-oriented and schedule-oriented basis. There is no question that the lowest level of a fully developed WBS comprises activities. However, it is more useful if one of the deliverable-oriented bases is used for the majority of the upper portion of the structure.

The following is an example of a WBS for an industrial complex (see Figure 2-2). To illustrate this example clearly, the division of elements at different junctures has been performed using different bases. It is important to note that if this project were to be implemented, a new all-deliverable WBS should be developed.

- ***Power House***
  —Steam generation system
  —Electrical generation system
  —Electrical transmission system
- ***Factory***
  —Receiving equipment
  —Processing equipment
  —Packaging equipment
  —Shipping equipment
- ***Office***
  —First floor
  —Second floor
  —Penthouse

FIGURE 2-2   Sample WBS

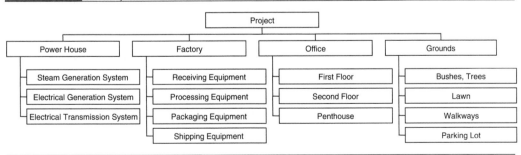

- *Grounds*
  —Phase One, bushes and trees
  —Phase Two, seeding for lawn
  —Phase Three, walkways
  —Phase Four, parking lot.

In this example, the breakdown basis for level one is physical location. The breakdown basis for the powerhouse is the functional system. The breakdown basis for the factory can be viewed as product, physical location, or functional system. The breakdown basis for the office is physical location. The breakdown basis for the grounds is sequential.

COMPARISON OF THE DIFFERENT BASES

The most common and easiest method of developing the WBS is to use the task, activity, or phase as the basis. The vast majority of elements in most WBSs fit this pattern. By and large, project professionals whose background is scheduling use this as the breakdown basis. It is fair to say that the transition from an activity-oriented WBS to a deliverable-oriented WBS is difficult for those who have developed task-oriented WBSs for a significant amount of time.

One stated advantage for schedule-oriented elements is that the resulting WBS can be used for many projects. Although this feature can be an advantage because the WBS is generic and not specific enough, it is also a disadvantage because the definitive features of the project are not addressed in a clear and highlighted fashion.

Another feature of schedule-oriented WBSs, which sometimes has been perceived as an advantage, is that the WBS is applicable when the project is not fully defined. Unfortunately, this becomes a disadvantage when the project is fully specified but the estimating and scheduling are still dependent on bundled estimates for items such as design, testing, etc.

Ultimately, because projects are carried out when people do things such as develop, draw, print, fix, fabricate, etc., the elements at the lowest level will always be activity-based. However, using the deliverable methodology changes the basis of division from deliverable-oriented to schedule-oriented as low in the WBS as possible.

The second most common basis of developing a WBS is the administrative basis. Project professionals who have a financial or administrative background tend to use disciplines, administrative units, or budget accounts as the basis of WBS breakdown. Although such bases would make tracking of funds very simple and straightforward, they may not significantly help the project management objectives. The bases included in the resource-oriented group—disciplines, administrative units, and financial accounts—should be used as little as possible, because these bases do not refer to the work but rather to the means by which the work is administered and paid for.

The most preferable bases are the deliverable-oriented bases: product, functional system, and physical area. It is very important to make sure that the elements on the first several levels of the WBS, especially those on level one, are deliverable-oriented and not schedule-oriented or resource-oriented. However, this does not mean that activities and costs are not important. On the contrary, a deliverable-oriented WBS that includes activities at the lowest levels results in a more meaningful analysis of the project schedule and project financing. For example, if the testing tasks are late, it would be possible to determine that complexity of testing the item BB has delayed the overall testing results. Similarly, if the costs are significantly below budget, it would be possible to determine that an unexpected reduction in component costs for item CC has caused this unexpected and favorable reduction.

PROCESS-ORIENTED PROJECTS

The point in the WBS at which the basis of division will change from deliverable-oriented to schedule-oriented depends on the nature of the project. If the project is deliverable-oriented, most of the divisions except the lowest level can be deliverables. If the project is process-oriented, most of the elements will be activities.

A project is deliverable-oriented if, at the end of the project, a unique final product is delivered to the client, such as a car, an airplane, a building, an organizational structure, or a set of design documents. By contrast, a process-oriented project is somewhat repetitious, such as running a lumber mill, a refinery, or a contamination cleanup project. In these cases, the project resembles a checklist of objectives that need to be estimated and scheduled.

The other distinction between a deliverable-oriented project and a process-oriented project is determined by testing whether or not the project activities are somewhat standardized, with repetition in developing replicas of the deliverable of the first project. To illustrate, designing and building the first supersonic jumbo jet is a deliverable-oriented project. However, manufacturing each of the next 245 planes is a process-oriented project. In some projects, where the physical deliverables are minimal or not commonly recognized as deliverables, the majority of elements are schedule-oriented.

Examples of these projects are cleanup of a contaminated site, demolition of a building, excavating the cavity for a building foundation, or removing a software virus from a computer program.

Additional examples of a deliverable-oriented project are:

- A new bank
- A new laboratory
- A new manufacturing plant
- A new software
- A software upgrade
- A unique facility design.

In contrast, examples of a process-oriented project are:

- Conducting annual closeout at a bank
- Converting chemicals to plastics
- Converting crude oil to gasoline
- Manufacturing a batch of chemicals
- Monitor productivity at Site G
- Issuing monthly payroll checks.

Deliverable-oriented projects have deliverable-oriented WBS elements for most of the project, with the exception of the lowest one or two levels. Those professionals who have developed schedule-oriented WBS exclusively may initially find it difficult to create deliverable-oriented WBS. Although such difficulty is minor for deliverable-oriented projects, it can be significant for process-oriented projects. Notwithstanding, a deliverable-oriented WBS is most useful in projects where it is more important to know the scope, cost, and duration of each delivered module rather than the activities that produced that module or group of modules.

Especially at the lower portion of the WBS, process-oriented projects tend to have schedule-oriented elements. It is difficult, although not impossible, and certainly advisable, to develop deliverable-oriented elements for the top levels of the WBS for a majority of the process-oriented projects. Notwithstanding, schedule-oriented WBSs are more appropriate for cost-plus projects, internal projects where there are no work packages to contract, and projects where the activities or the-step-by-step process is of utmost importance.

Successful project management depends on well-defined and fully implemented OBSs, RBSs, and WBSs. Using these planning tools, a successful project depends on clear planning, accurate reporting, and regular updating. Deliverable-oriented elements can be developed for the top levels of the WBSs for most projects. This methodical approach initially requires extra effort for those who have used schedule-oriented WBSs in the past. Once this methodology becomes second nature, deliverable-oriented WBSs can be developed with ease.

ORGANIZATIONAL PRIORITIES

Sometimes there is a tendency to add items to the WBS that do not represent a deliverable but that are activities that are part of the organizational priorities and imperatives. The intent of including such items in the first level of WBS is to signal conformance with organizational imperatives or to maintain organizational harmony. The items that often find their way to the first level of WBS include:

- User support
- Purchasing
- Integration
- Systems engineering
- Value engineering
- Contract process

- Project monitoring
- Project management
- Budget approval
- Project closeout
- Reporting
- Design process.

The rationale for not including these items at level one is two-fold. First, it would distort the basis of division at level one, which otherwise is deliverable-oriented. Second, and more importantly, placement of such activities at level one would detract from the accuracy of the plans, distorting the sharp focus necessary for monitoring the schedule and cost.

An example of such a WBS modification was observed during development for a project whose objective was to deliver a computer system to a customer. This project involved providing software and hardware to the client at the end of the project. The elements of this WBS were deliverable-oriented through level four (see Figure 2-3). The level one WBS items were:

- Hardware
- Software
- System documents.

After the WBS was developed, the project manager was instructed by the supervising divisional manager to add user support as a level one element. The reason was that there was a transition in the organization toward more user-friendly systems development. Insertion of user support as a level one WBS item was intended to recognize and highlight this priority. Therefore, the level one elements of this systems development (see Figure 2-4) WBS became:

- Hardware
- Software

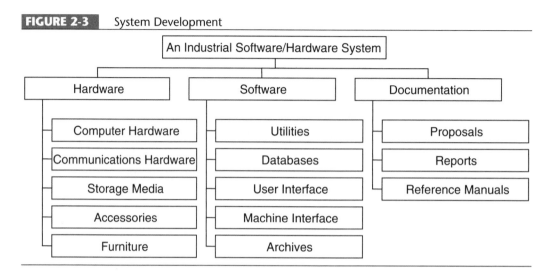

FIGURE 2-3 System Development

- System documents
- User support.

The disadvantage of listing these activities as level one items is that they become freestanding activities that seemingly are not associated with any specific product. Certainly, these activities are needed to deliver the products that are listed on level three or level four of the WBS, and therefore, they need to be listed. Moreover, even if these activities are listed at lower levels, they can be summarized across WBS, RBS, or OBS lines. The only difference is that they are not highlighted at level one of the WBS. Again, such

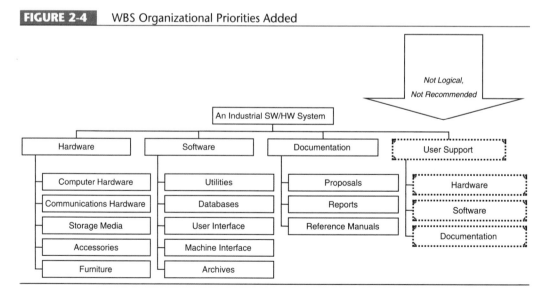

FIGURE 2-4 WBS Organizational Priorities Added

augmentation of the WBS distorts the logical structure of the WBS, and therefore, is not recommended.

SEMANTICS

Using vague or multiple-meaning words as WBS titles can cause confusion and misunderstandings in the interpretation and planning of the WBS items. For example, if a WBS item is labeled as *procurement*, it could refer to the people who buy things, the department that employs them, or the process of buying things. Similarly, if a WBS item is labeled as *mechanical*, it could refer to the mechanical engineering design process, the mechanical portion of the deliverables, the mechanical engineers, or the department that employs them. Similarly, if a WBS item is labeled as *system*, it could refer to the system that is delivered to the client, the software portion of the system, the people who write the software, the department that employs them, or the process of writing software.

The probability of confusion and misunderstanding is minimized if these words are interpreted within the appropriate context. However, it is incumbent on the project planner to make every effort to eliminate all potential causes of confusion from the project plans.

As an example, consider a project that is described by the following WBS components: procurement, systems, civil, mechanical, and legal. These elements could be interpreted as uniformly referring to disciplines, administrative units, activities, or not uniformly referring to a collage of the above (see Figure 2-5). Notwithstanding, if there is a possibility of ambiguity in naming the WBS elements, qualifiers should be used such as mechanical engineering department, civil engineers, procurement phase II, software module, mechanical drawings, or contract documents. Although not using

FIGURE 2-5   Ambiguity

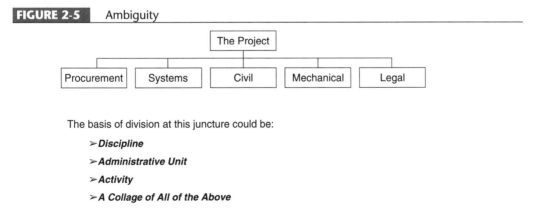

The basis of division at this juncture could be:

➢ *Discipline*

➢ *Administrative Unit*

➢ *Activity*

➢ *A Collage of All of the Above*

these qualifiers might not have caused confusion, using these qualifiers virtually ensures no chance of misinterpreting the meaning of the item labels.

CHANGING THE PARADIGM

Sometimes, it is possible to change a WBS from schedule-oriented to deliverable-oriented by modifying some elements and by changing the wording of some of the elements. However, the transition from a schedule-oriented WBS to a deliverable-oriented WBS is not simply using nonaction words, but rather involves looking at the project from the standpoint of the client. Therefore, the WBS would include the elements that the client is interested in receiving and those that the client will pay for. Consequently, as the client changes the scope and schedule constraints of various modules, it would be very easy to determine and justify the impact of such changes on the cost and schedule of the project.

As the WBS is developed, the project management professionals should be careful not to infuse details of how the work will be delivered into the description of the deliverable itself. To effectively achieve this, it is necessary to develop an RBS and an OBS before starting to divide the project objectives.

The transition from a schedule-oriented WBS or a resource-oriented WBS to a deliverable-oriented WBS should be guided by the objectives, scope, and specifications of the project. In cases where the objectives are not fully developed at the time of WBS development, one can develop only the first two or three levels of the WBS. Later, as more project information becomes available, the WBS can be expanded and refined.

Conceptually, the process of developing a deliverable-oriented WBS is relatively simple. The project is divided into components that, when combined, will produce the final project deliverable. Ideally, one would avoid listing activities and tasks until the last one or two levels of the WBS. The emphasis would be placed on describing the components that produce the project, the modules that would produce the component, the units that would produce the module, etc. It is advisable to avoid listing the personnel responsible for delivery of reports, evaluations, reports, or products. Such resource assignments can be done easily and systematically once the WBS and RBS are established, preferably independent of each other.

The following is the first level of a WBS that was developed using the traditional schedule-oriented mindset (see Figure 2-6):

Level One
- Conceptual design

FIGURE 2-6   Schedule-Oriented WBS

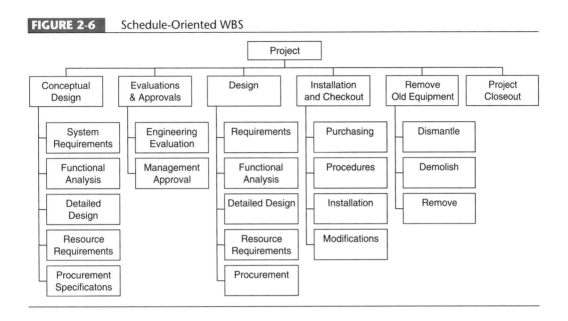

- Evaluation and approvals
- Design
- Installation and checkout
- Removal of old equipment
- Project closeout.

To illustrate this example further, the level two breakdown for the design branch is shown here:

Level Two, Design

- System requirements
- Functional analysis
- Detailed design
- Resource requirements
- Procurement specifications.

Since schedule-oriented WBSs tend to be entirely activity-based, it is very difficult if not impossible to discern what the objective of the project is and what its deliverables are. Although not clearly identified in the WBS, the objective of this project is to deliver the following:

- Two new emission stacks
- New emissions monitoring system
- Emergency power building.

By contrast, a deliverable-based WBS (see Figure 2-7) would be constructed along the following lines:

FIGURE 2-7 Deliverable-Oriented WBS

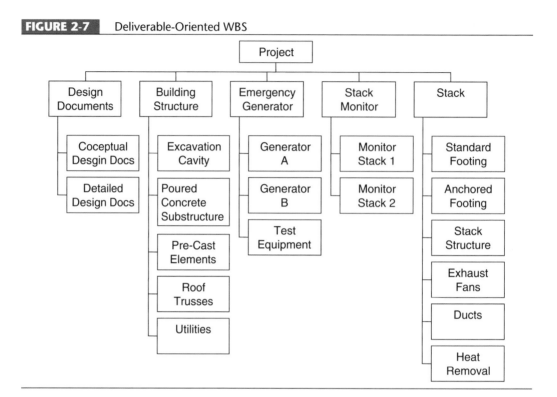

Level One
- Design documents
- Building structure
- Emergency generator system
- Stack monitors
- Stacks.

This WBS clearly describes what the client expects from the project manager or the contractor when the project is finished. Accordingly, tracking the project's progress would be relatively simple—by noting the progress of the delivery of the project's components.

To illustrate this WBS further, the level two items will be shown here also:

Level Two, Design Documents
- Conceptual documents
- Detailed design documents.

Level Two, Building Structure
- Excavation cavity
- Poured-concrete substructures

- Pre-cast-concrete elements
- Roof trusses
- Utilities.

Level Two, Generator
- Generator A
- Generator B
- Test equipment.

Level Two, Stack Monitors
- Monitor for stack A
- Monitor for stack B.

Level Two, Stacks
- Standard footing
- Anchored footing
- Stack structure
- Exhaust fans
- Ducts
- Heat removal system.

Depending on the size of the project and the traditions of this particular environment, the next level of activities might be schedule-oriented.

This example illustrates that with the deliverable-oriented WBS, one can easily and clearly follow the progress of the project components. One gets a clear idea of the project objectives and what is involved in achieving those objectives. A deliverable-oriented WBS is easier to schedule, estimate, and monitor. Planning a project with a deliverable-oriented WBS is conducted by planning specific items that make up the project and is not based on planning generic activities involved in delivering them in a bundled fashion. Equally important, when the time comes to make those inevitable changes to the project plan, the changes are made more accurately and logically because the changes are implemented only in those items that were affected by the change.

A carefully organized WBS will set the foundation for planning the details of logical and integrated project data for the benefit of all other aspects of the project, and particularly for the benefit of estimating and scheduling. A well-defined deliverable-oriented WBS will facilitate unambiguous planning, accurate reporting, and regular updating. Deliverable-oriented elements can be developed for the top levels of the WBS for most projects with relative ease. Although development of deliverable-oriented WBS elements at lower levels may initially require some extra effort for those who have used schedule-oriented WBS in the past, deliverable-oriented WBSs can be developed with nominal effort once this process becomes second nature for the project management professional.

CHAPTER 3

Resource Breakdown Structure

T he practice of formalizing the resource pool falls at the interface between general management and project management. The resource breakdown structure (RBS) has its analog in the well-known work breakdown structure (WBS). In the few organizations that use variations of an RBS, project managers are able to plan the project with greater assurance of the resource data reliability. In other words, the project manager can depend on this structure to determine the amount of resources at-hand and their estimated cost in order to capitalize on organizational memory with respect to project resources. In some cases, the project manager might modify and use an RBS previously prepared by those charged with accounting for the organization's resources. To use it well, the RBS must be kept up to date, and its resource contents and their costs must be accurate.

Managers have a long history of dividing anticipated project work into smaller parcels and presenting the resulting schema graphically. This "breaking down" of the work facilitates better management in many ways. Similarly, in-house project resources should be examined methodically at the earliest opportunity through the creation of the RBS. This structure will greatly facilitate the resource assignments and scheduling in this project and similar ones that use these resources.

Early in the project's planning stage, the project manager should be provided a detailed listing of the available resources, including project-specific resources obtainable from outside the organization. The term *resources* refers to everything that will cost money to obtain and is necessary for the completion of the project, such as labor, equipment, licenses, and taxes.

If the initial resource estimate is prepared correctly, the proportional cost of each component of the deliverable can be understood easily even during the early stages of the project, albeit the structure and values may not be exceptionally accurate. Equally important, the continual improvements

---

This chapter was jointly authored by Parviz F. Rad and Denis F. Cioffi.

that this estimate must undergo can proceed formally using the formalized RBS. The estimate will be easy to review and improve as more information becomes available. Then, as the almost inevitable changes of scope occur, further modifications to the estimate can be made formally, easily, and clearly. Therefore, every change to the project cost can be justified and defended with detailed data.

NOMENCLATURE, DIMENSIONS, AND UNITS

The word *rate* carries its usual meaning of some quantity measured per unit time, e.g., a worker's cost rate could be measured in dollars per hour. If one needs to discuss the expense of individual items, e.g., cans of paint, the cost is not a rate but simply so many dollars per can; the unit may be called *each*.

Effort equals the product of workers and time, measured then in worker-hours, worker-days, worker-months, or worker-years. At any given point in the project, the effort divided by the appropriate unit of time equals the number of workers. For example, if a project requires an effort of 100 worker-years, completion over a year's duration would require 100 workers; however, to be completed in six months (i.e., 0.5 years), 200 workers would be needed. (This illustration ignores the effect of compression and expansion on the cost, which will be discussed later in this book.)

The number of resources that would be present during the execution of a given task, or the "instantaneous" worker need, will be called the *resource intensity* for the task. It is this intensity that will become the input to the mechanism by which the overloading of resources is determined, which might in turn trigger a resource leveling.

Because workers are paid for their effort, even in internal projects, they represent an expense to the enterprise, and therefore, internal resource effort should be viewed as equivalent to cost. Units must be retained in such arithmetic, whether explicitly or implicitly, so that the translation from effort to cost occurs through the cost rate per worker, e.g., worker-hours multiplied by dollars per hour per worker yields dollars. Figures 3-1 and 3-2 show schematic representations of estimating the cost of using personnel or equipment over some duration. If three workers are used for four days, we have used 12 worker days. Multiplying by the cost rate yields the cost for that effort. Calculating the cost of equipment is similar except that the effort is measured in equipment days.

One makes estimates through this conversion. That is, if in shorthand notation one speaks of estimating an element of the WBS, ultimately the

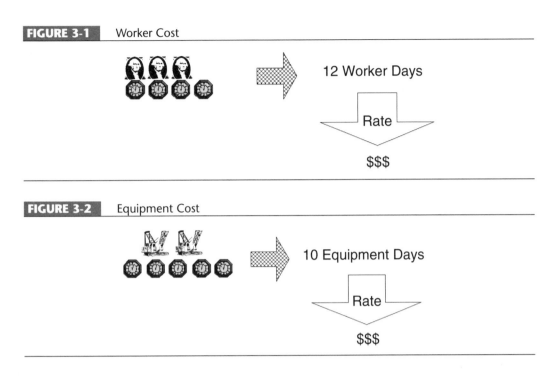

FIGURE 3-1 Worker Cost

12 Worker Days

Rate

$$$

FIGURE 3-2 Equipment Cost

10 Equipment Days

Rate

$$$

cost is desired, but in the first—sometimes hidden (or skipped!)—step, one must estimate the effort.

RESOURCE BREAKDOWN STRUCTURE

An RBS classifies and catalogs the resources needed to accomplish project objectives. Just as the WBS does for the deliverable elements of a project, the RBS is able to provide a consistent framework for dividing the resources into small units for planning, estimating, and managing. Figure 3-3

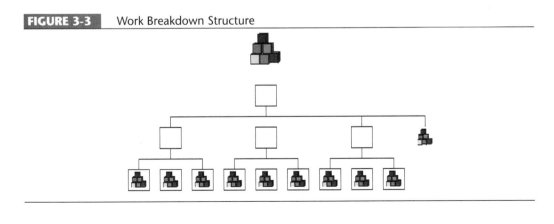

FIGURE 3-3 Work Breakdown Structure

shows a schematic representation of the familiar work breakdown structure; the project deliverable, at the top, has been broken into many smaller deliverables. Figure 3-4 is the schematic representation of the RBS for the same project. In many ways, the RBS is analogous to the WBS and claims similar advantages in improving communication, integration, planning, and estimating.

An RBS differs from other human resource or budgeting classification methods because it applies directly to project management, and not to, for example, cost accounting or personnel evaluations. Rather than developing a new RBS for each project, the organization can develop various RBSs for families of projects. As project managers plan each new project, they select

FIGURE 3-4   Resource Breakdown Structure

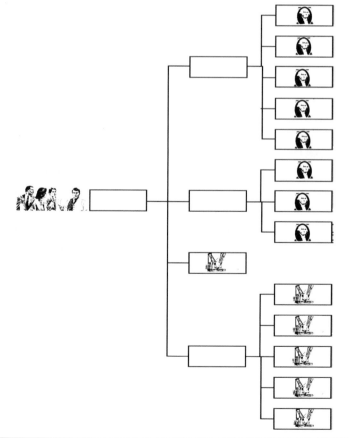

only those portions of the common RBS that apply to the project. Here, the WBS and the RBS work together, mapping a project's WBS onto the RBS and then linking project activities with specific available resources.

RBS DEVELOPMENT

To reiterate, one does not plan a project while developing the RBS. Instead, the RBS tabulates the resources available or needed for projects of a certain type or even for a specific project. To develop the RBS, it is necessary to begin by dividing the pool of resources into entities specific enough so that this structure can serve as a shopping catalog for resources that are necessary to accomplish project activities developed in the WBS.

Similar to the WBS, developing an RBS involves grouping all resources in three to nine categories in level one. Then each of the level one items is subdivided, and so forth. Consistency in the division bases remains a crucial component of the structure. Ideally, the rationale that divides one level from the next should be consistent across all elements and branches of the RBS; however, at a minimum, the division basis at any juncture must be the same for all parts of the project.

The division process continues until one has identified discrete, manageable resource items. A useful guide is to keep dividing the resource pool until the lowest level items reflect the resource details that interest the estimators and schedulers. Again, this level of detail varies among companies and project managers. The nature of the resource pool and its administrative environment determine the depths of the levels. Notwithstanding, one must maintain a reasonable consistency in the degree of detail of the lowest level elements.

The RBS explicitly contains both the unit of measurement for each resource (e.g., foot, pound, cubic yard, equipment-hour, labor-hour) and the cost of a single unit of the resource (e.g., $10,000 per equipment-hour). Items that get used entirely in a project can be measured as *each*, for example, installed motors, doors, computers, hard disks, and so forth. The RBS may list either direct costs or total costs including overhead, but all resource costs should be listed with identical or consistent measurement units, with or without overhead.

As a reminder of the importance of consistency in measurement units (and many other consistencies), consider the example of the Mars Climate Orbiter, which failed in September 1999 because one navigating group worked in English units and the other in metric units.[1] A much tighter consistency than this minimum requirement of working in the same system is desirable. For example, the measurement for all time-related elements can be one of hours, days, months, or years, but the chosen unit should appear in all appropriate quantities (unless the numbers become unreasonably large or small). The same statement can be made about all other dimensions and combinations of dimensions involved in the project, e.g., length (inches, feet, yards, centimeters, meters, kilometers) or volume (gallons, cubic yards, cubic centimeters, cubic meters).

Limited resources mentioned, for example, might include 14 civil engineers available for a new project, or 2 cranes, or 35 brick layers, or 4 programmers, or 3 photographers. On the other hand, for high-priority projects, some resources may be limitless. The project environment may be such that it would allow, for example, as many CAD operators as demanded by the project, or contract officers, or safety engineers. As with the WBS, the RBS can be presented graphically, in a tabular fashion or using indented text.

THE PRIMARY DIVISION BASIS

The best (although not necessarily the only) lines of demarcation among the elements at the first level of the RBS are:
- People (labor)
- Tools, machinery
- Materials and installed equipment
- Fees, licenses.

The labor category is often referred to as human resources. It includes skill categories, professional disciplines, and work functions. All possible human resources should be listed here, regardless of their physical location, administrative attachment, or contractual circumstances. Figure 3-5 shows the categorization of human resources along organizational lines in anticipation of future plans involving allocation of funds and/or assignment of personnel from different organizational entities.

Tools and machinery are those physical items needed by project team members to perform their duties successfully. When the project ends, the project team will remove the tools and machinery from the project environment. Examples of items in this category are testing equipment, hand tools, equipment to install project deliverables, and computers to monitor and evaluate the installation process. These items are usually leased or rented. Purchasing this type of item can be more cost-effective for lengthy projects, but ultimately these items will still be removed from the project site.

FIGURE 3-5   Sample RBS

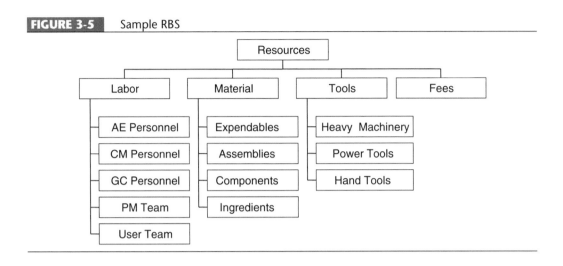

For planning and cost estimating, sometimes the leasing agency rolls the wages of the operator into the rental fee of the equipment. Consequently, when tools and machinery are rented or leased, some organizations treat the operators as an integral part of the physical equipment. This practice blurs the line between the human and physical resources.

Installed equipment and materials are purchased for the project and ultimately installed, integrated, and embedded in the project deliverables. Examples include fiber-optic cables, furniture, tape drives, monitoring equipment, pumps, ducts, and computers.

Fees and licenses refer to those cost items that do not involve any implementation or installation but are required for the execution of the project. Examples include insurance policies, bond agreements, permit fees, license charges, and taxes.

Complications arise when the client provides some combination of equipment, funding, and personnel. Although in such cases the detailed solution varies depending on the project and the priorities of the organizations involved, the most general approach still lists all necessary project resources in the RBS regardless of how they will be funded. Once the total project cost estimate is prepared, the client-furnished equipment and labor costs can be subtracted from the resources requested by the project manager or the contractor. Figure 3-6 shows the RBS for the stack monitor project described in the Chapter 2.

Money is not considered a resource in this breakdown structure. Money represents the primary means by which resources are provided. To illustrate

FIGURE 3-6   RBS Example

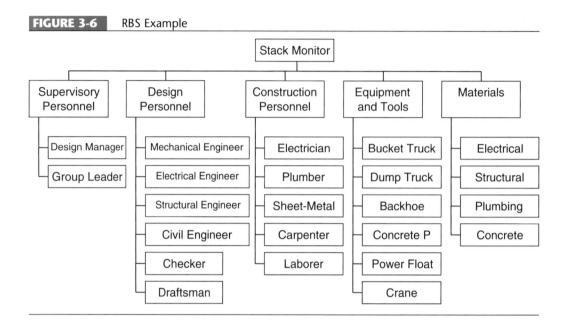

the validity of this concept, consider that for internal projects, money is often not the exchange medium. Although resources such as worker hours or equipment may be granted directly, the project manager should still regard them as resources to be listed in the RBS—resources whose cost will be absorbed by the enterprise, implicitly or explicitly.

After the mapping of the WBS onto the RBS, which is represented schematically in Figure 3-7, the money necessary for the project is estimated through the sum of the products of two numbers: the resource quantities demanded by the WBS and the corresponding RBS unit costs. That is, for each element at the lowest level of the WBS, the desired quantity of the resource is multiplied by its cost per unit of appropriate measure to yield the cost. Because multiplication is often considered implicitly, the sum of the resource estimates from the WBS is equivalent to the total cost estimate.

LOWER-LEVEL DIVISION BASES WITH A CONCENTRATION ON HUMAN RESOURCES

One can categorize equipment, supplies, tools, and material by size, function, cost, or technical area. Fees can be divided by type or by cost. Aside from these general guidelines, equipment, materials, and fees are highly discipline-dependent and must be dealt with on a project-by-project basis.

FIGURE 3-7   Elemental Estimate

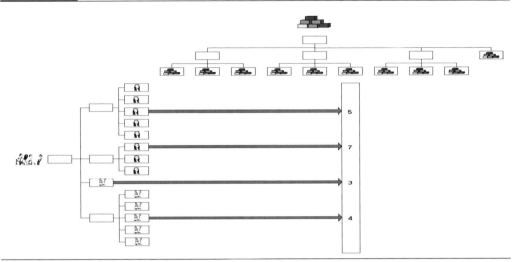

However, the categorization of people deserves a bit of amplification, because it is common to all projects, and because people are the most important resource in any project. Nearly 40–50 percent of the cost of construction and industrial projects is attributable to labor costs. The cost of human resources is approximately 75 percent of the cost of systems and software development projects.[2–4]

Ideally, the project manager plans, estimates, and manages all tasks and resources independent of where the resources reside, administratively or physically. Accordingly, if a human resource item is part of an outside organization that the project manager intends to hire for an individual task, then that task and its associated resources should not be regarded as part of the project at hand. If the project manager does not have managerial authority over a certain resource, then he or she has no major influence in the use of the resource. Therefore, the resource and the resulting product are aptly termed *outsourced.*

The level of detail to which human resources are defined in an RBS depends on the organization, the project, and to some extent, the individual project manager. But with that obvious caveat stated, we now consider further the transition from one human resource RBS level to the next, which should occur on one of the following bases:

- Administrative unit
- Physical location

- Credential (in a particular discipline)
- Work function
- Position title
- Skill level.

Organizational managers sometimes divide human resources on the basis of their administrative affiliations, such as company A, contractor X, or organization D. In other cases, it might be preferable to catalog the resources into groups based on physical location, especially as it relates to proximity to the project site, e.g., human resources from Los Angeles, Boston, southern plants, or western contractors.

The *credential discipline basis* is used when people need to be identified with their degree specializations, their certifications, or other recognized credentials. Examples of these divisions include individuals with a degree in chemistry, professional engineer's license, CPA certification, or master's degree. A *work function basis* is used when managers must know workers' functions, independent of their specialized degrees. Examples of such divisions are programmers, test technicians, supervisors, team leaders, equipment operators, designers, estimators, and project control specialists.

Position title basis is required when, independent of credentials or job functions, the positions individuals hold in the organizational hierarchy determine their duties in the project. Examples of such divisions are contract officers, program directors, department chiefs, and divisional vice-presidents. Finally, when it is appropriate to classify project personnel by their degree of effectiveness and skill, project managers can use the skill basis, e.g., expert, skilled, semi-skilled. Naturally, the skill designation should always be used in conjunction with credential or function designations.

Again, for best results, a reasonable level of consistency must be maintained in grouping the resources. Regardless of whether labor items are categorized by degree, job title, or job function, the categorization should be consistent across all labor items at that level of the RBS.

ESTIMATING THE COSTS

The diagram shown in Figure 3-7 captures the essentials of using the WBS and RBS in tandem. One begins at the lowest level of the WBS, which is denoted as Level N. The cost of each element is calculated by multiplying the quantity of resources required by its unit cost obtained from the RBS. It is important to note that details are not hidden. The category of the resource, its intensity, and its duration are clearly indicated as part of this calculation.

For example, if a project needs three brick layers for four days to build a wall, then the category is brick layer, the intensity is 3 workers, the duration is 4 days, and the effort is 12 worker-days. At a unit cost of $300 per worker per day, the cost is $3600.

The project's total cost can be found by adding all these costs together, but so many numbers are somewhat unwieldy, and such a calculation hides additional information that subsequently can be obtained easily. Therefore, in the next step, one moves up a level to determine—by simple addition—the total quantity of resources necessary for all elements at level N-1, grouped by resource category. The process repeats, proceeding from bottom to top, until each element of the WBS shows the total resources it requires, grouped by resource category. Once the calculations are extended to the level zero, the project's total cost has been determined, as has the cost of all intermediate elements of the WBS. In addition to the cost, we now have the resource utilization values for all subunits defined in the WBS.

As in any method of estimating, it is necessary to check the estimate against experiential data and against the subjective knowledge of management professionals. The first key question to ask at this point is: Is the estimate for the total cost of the project reasonable? Poor overall estimates often result from inadvertent omissions of key elements in the WBS and the RBS. Therefore, correction primarily involves filling the logical gaps in the WBS by enhancing, or adding to, the current elements. Correction may also involve improving elemental estimates at the lowest levels, but an elemental estimate should not be changed arbitrarily from what is believed to be the best estimate. Further, the estimate values for those items above Level N, i.e., those items that are parents of lower-level items, should not be changed. The reason is that all parents' estimates are derived from sums of lower-level estimates, not from direct input.

Project planning documents, including the estimate, should be treated as living documents. As new information becomes available, the WBS, RBS, estimates, and schedule must be updated and, hopefully, refined. Ideally, these enhancements should be conducted frequently rather than only for specific administrative milestones and budget deadlines. At every update opportunity, the enhanced WBS (and if necessary, an enhanced RBS) should be used to refine the elemental estimates.

A well-defined, accurate, consistent, and regularly updated WBS and RBS will significantly improve the likelihood of project success by facilitating clear plans and good communication. With these two planning tools, a manager can make a systematic and accurate estimate of the project's required resources—and therefore, its cost. Once deliverable-oriented WBS elements have been developed for a project, producing a cost estimate becomes a simple matter of mapping the WBS onto the RBS and assigning the appropriate resources to the individual WBS elements. This methodical approach initially requires some extra effort, but if an organization regularly produces and maintains its RBS families, the process becomes second nature. The project manager's anxiety about cost estimating will decrease, and the organization will achieve significant efficiencies in planning, scheduling, and monitoring.

Using a good WBS with an accurate RBS, it is possible to ask detailed cost and resource questions about the project, such as:

- What is the total number of worker-hours needed for module A?
- How many worker-hours of chemists do we need for modules A, B, and C?

When these elemental and total estimates are combined with a good schedule, it is possible to ask questions combining detailed time and resource issues, such as:

- How many programmers do we need for the entire project in July?
- How many engineers do we need for module C during July?
- Would the demand for client-side programmers be reduced next July if we postponed module B by three months?
- How many more analysts would we need next February if the scope of module D were doubled?
- How would doubling the scope of module G affect project cost, schedule, and resource requirements?
- If Module F were delayed six months, what would the resulting cost and schedule look like?

DETAILED EXAMPLE

Figure 3-8 shows a graphic representation of the top levels of an RBS that was developed for a system development project in one of the author's classes. The full RBS included one more level below what is graphically shown here, although what is shown here will illustrate a fully developed RBS. Figure 3-9 is a graphic representation of the first two levels of the WBS. Figures 3-10 and 3-11 are tabular representations of the WBS and RBS for the same project. Figure 3-12 shows the assignment of resources to the elements on the lowest level. Figure 3-13 shows the roll-up of costs and resources for a level one item. Finally, Figure 3-14 shows the resource requirements, and the corresponding cost estimate, for the top level, which is the total project.

FIGURE 3-8 RBS for System Development

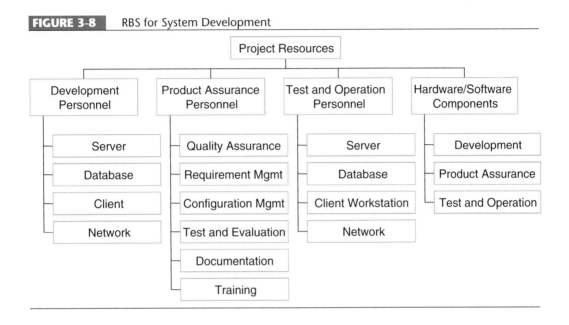

FIGURE 3-9 WBS Example

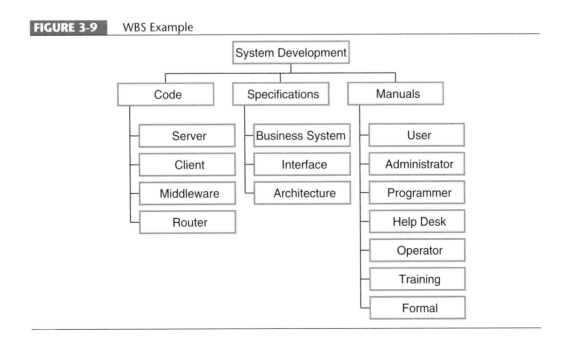

FIGURE 3-10 WBS Detail

000 System							
	100 System Code						
		110 Server Code					
			111 Server Source Code				
			112 Server Object Code				
		120 Client Code					
			121 Client Source Code				
			122 Client Object Code				
		130 Middleware Code					
			131 Middleware Source Code				
			132 Middleware Object Code				
		140 Router Tables					
			141 Internal Routing Tables				
			142 External Routing Tables				
	200 System Specifications						
		210 Business System and Technical Design					
			211 System Requirements				
			212 System Boundary				
			213 Version Definition				
		220 Interface Design Definition					
			221 Data Interchange Requirements				
			222 Interfacing Protocols				
		230 Implementation Level Architecture					
			231 Server Architecture				

FIGURE 3-11 RBS Sample

						Unit of Measure	Cost/Price	
							(Dollars)	
R100 Development Staff								
	R110 Server Development Personnel							
		R111 Systems Analyst				Staff Hour	$70	
		R112 Application Analyst				Staff Hour	$60	
		R113 Systems Programmer				Staff Hour	$50	
	R120 Database Development Personnel							
		R121 Data Base Administrator				Staff Hour	$75	
		R122 Sr. Data Design Specialist				Staff Hour	$65	
		R123 Data Design Specialist				Staff Hour	$60	
	R130 Client Development Personnel							
		R131 PC Systems Analyst				Staff Hour	$65	
		R132 PC Systems Programmer				Staff Hour	$55	
	R140 Network Development Personnel							
		R141 Infrastructure Analyst				Staff Hour	$85	
		R142 Infrastructure Engineer				Staff Hour	$80	
		R143 Network Engineer				Staff Hour	$70	
R200 Product Assurance Staff								
	R210 Quality Assurance Personnel							
		R211 Sr. QA Specialist				Staff Hour	$65	
		R212 QA Specialist				Staff Hour	$45	
	R220 Requirements Management Personnel							
		R221 Requirements Manager				Staff Hour	$65	
		R222 Requirements Specialist				Staff Hour	$45	
	R230 Configuration Management Personnel							

FIGURE 3-12 Elemental Estimate

	Unit	Intensity	Duration (Days)	Total (Staff Hours)	Unit Cost	Extension
000 System						**$2,426,760**
100 System Code						**$966,400**
110 Server Code						**$373,160**
111 Server Source Code						**$345,600**
R121 Data Base Administrator	Staff Hour	1	100	800	$75	$60,000
R122 Sr. Data Design Specialist	Staff Hour	1	125	1000	$65	$65,000
R123 Data Design Specialist	Staff Hour	3	125	3000	$60	$180,000
R241 Test Manager	Staff Hour	1	10	80	$70	$5,600
R242 Sr. Test Engineer	Staff Hour	1	25	200	$65	$13,000
R243 Test Engineer	Staff Hour	1	50	400	$55	$22,000
112 Server Object Code						**$27,560**
R121 Data Base Administrator	Staff Hour	1	6	48	$75	$3,600
R122 Sr. Data Design Specialist	Staff Hour	1	12	96	$65	$6,240
R123 Data Design Specialist	Staff Hour	1	24	192	$60	$11,520
R231 Sr. CM Specialist	Staff Hour	1	5	40	$65	$2,600
R232 CM Specialist	Staff Hour	1	10	80	$45	$3,600
120 Client Code						**$139,200**
121 Client Source Code						**$124,600**
R131 PC Systems Analyst	Staff Hour	1	75	600	$65	$39,000
R132 PC Systems Programmer	Staff Hour	2	75	1200	$55	$66,000
R241 Test Manager	Staff Hour	1	5	40	$70	$2,800
R242 Sr. Test Engineer	Staff Hour	1	12	96	$65	$6,240
R243 Test Engineer	Staff Hour	1	24	192	$55	$10,560
122 Client Object Code						**$14,600**
R131 PC Systems Analyst	Staff Hour	1	6	48	$65	$3,120
R132 PC Systems Programmer	Staff Hour	1	12	96	$55	$5,280
R231 Sr. CM Specialist	Staff Hour	1	5	40	$65	$2,600
R232 CM Specialist	Staff Hour	1	10	80	$45	$3,600
130 Middleware Code						**$294,040**

FIGURE 3-13 Project Resource and Cost Estimate—Level One Items

Level 1 Resource Requirements					
000 System					**$2,414,360**
100 System Code					**$969,400**
R111 Systems Analyst	Staff Hour		848	$70	$59,360
R112 Application Analyst	Staff Hour		1104	$60	$66,240
R113 Systems Programmer	Staff Hour		2136	$50	$106,800
R121 Data Base Administrator	Staff Hour		848	$75	$63,600
R122 Sr. Data Design Specialist	Staff Hour		1104	$65	$71,760
R123 Data Design Specialist	Staff Hour		3192	$60	$191,520
R131 PC Systems Analyst	Staff Hour		648	$65	$42,120
R132 PC Systems Programmer	Staff Hour		1296	$55	$71,280
R141 Infrastructure Analyst	Staff Hour		640	$85	$54,400
R142 Infrastructure Engineer	Staff Hour		640	$80	$51,200
R143 Network Engineer	Staff Hour		640	$70	$44,800
R231 Sr. CM Specialist	Staff Hour		160	$65	$10,400
R232 Configuration Management Specialist	Staff Hour		200	$45	$9,000
R241 Test Manager	Staff Hour		216	$70	$15,120
R242 Sr. Test Engineer	Staff Hour		664	$65	$43,160
R243 Test Engineer	Staff Hour		1248	$55	$68,640
200 System Specifications					**$775,000**
R111 Systems Analyst	Staff Hour		2560	$70	$179,200
R112 Application Analyst	Staff Hour		1920	$60	$115,200
R121 Data Base Administrator	Staff Hour		320	$75	$24,000
R122 Sr. Data Design Specialist	Staff Hour		640	$65	$41,600
R123 Data Design Specialist	Staff Hour		640	$60	$38,400
R131 PC Systems Analyst	Staff Hour		320	$65	$20,800

FIGURE 3-14   Project Resource and Cost Estimate—Project Level

Level 0 Resource Requirements						
000 System						$2,414,360
R111 Systems Analyst			Staff Hour	4888	$70	$342,160
R112 Application Analyst			Staff Hour	4224	$60	$253,440
R113 Systems Programmer			Staff Hour	2136	$50	$106,800
R121 Data Base Administrator			Staff Hour	1808	$75	$135,600
R122 Sr. Data Design Specialist			Staff Hour	2984	$65	$193,960
R123 Data Design Specialist			Staff Hour	4712	$60	$282,720
R131 PC Systems Analyst			Staff Hour	2448	$65	$159,120
R132 PC Systems Programmer			Staff Hour	1696	$55	$93,280
R141 Infrastructure Analyst			Staff Hour	1280	$85	$108,800
R142 Infrastructure Engineer			Staff Hour	1280	$80	$102,400
R143 Network Engineer			Staff Hour	1280	$70	$89,600
R221 Requirements Manager			Staff Hour	240	$65	$15,600
R222 Requirements Specialist			Staff Hour	320	$45	$14,400
R231 Sr. CM Specialist			Staff Hour	160	$65	$10,400
R231 Sr. Configuration Management Specialist			Staff Hour	200	$45	$9,000
R241 Test Manager			Staff Hour	216	$70	$15,120
R242 Sr. Test Engineer			Staff Hour	664	$65	$43,160
R243 Test Engineer			Staff Hour	1248	$55	$68,640
R251 Documentation Manager			Staff Hour	1088	$50	$54,400
R252 Sr. Documentation Specialist			Staff Hour	1848	$45	$83,160
R253 Documentation Specialist			Staff Hour	3640	$40	$145,600
R261 Sr. Training Specialist			Staff Hour	120	$45	$5,400

Development of a resource breakdown structure uses an analogue of the logic and philosophy that are used in the development of a WBS. An RBS categorizes and tabulates the resource pool that is available—or should be available—to the project. An RBS will provide a systematic and formalized tool for calculating the cost of individual resources that are needed for each task of the project. Summarizing these costs across all resources will result in detailed estimates for the project on a resource-by-resource basis. Additionally, summarizing such costs across WBS elements will provide cost details for each of the project's deliverables. The availability of detailed resource costs will significantly improve the accuracy of the estimate. More importantly, the RBS will facilitate analysis of the changes to project cost that are the result of inevitable changes in the project's environment.

NOTES

1. R.A. Kerr, A System Fails at Mars, A Spacecraft Is Lost, *Science* 286 (November 19, 1999): 1457-1459.

2. Anonymous, *Parametric Estimating Handbook*, 2nd ed. (Washington, DC: US Department of Defense, 1999).

3. Anonymous, *Skills and Knowledge of Cost Engineering*, 4th ed. (Morgantown, WV: Association for Advancement of Cost Engineering—AACE, 1999).

4. M.R. Vigder, and A.W. Kark, *Software Cost Estimation and Control* (Ottawa, Ontario, Canada: National Research Council of Canada, February 1994).

CHAPTER 4

Estimating Models

The most accurate and most reliable estimate for a project can be developed when all the elements of the work breakdown structure (WBS) have been identified with a reasonable degree of reliability and when the resource breakdown structure (RBS) has been defined with the desired degree of certainty. This estimate is referred to as the *bottom-up estimate* and it is derived from detailed information that is contained in the WBS and RBS at the time of the estimate. Unfortunately, the amount of detail required for such an estimate is not available until a major portion of the project has been designed and implemented. Notwithstanding, the project stakeholders must have indications of the cost and duration of the project to be able to approve the project for the earliest stages of implementation. Therefore, an abbreviated version of WBS and RBS must be developed during the inception stages in order to formulate a rough estimate of cost and duration of the project for preliminary decision purposes.

As the information in these structures is enhanced and expanded in line with available project detail, the project estimate will become more reliable. Depending on the organization, the first estimate is sometimes called *conceptual* or *order of magnitude*. This first estimate can be developed using any one of the models described here, although the analogous estimating technique is most often used for conceptual estimates.

Availability of historical data is paramount in the development and use of estimating models, as well as in the general process of estimating. Historical data provide a basis for more a reliable estimate during the early stages and for more detailed and realistic plans during the detailed planning stages. Historical project data for construction and industrial projects span several decades and a multitude of project types under numerous implementation constraints.

Unfortunately, software projects do not enjoy the same luxury, particularly since many software and system development projects are regarded as vastly different from those in the historical database. In addition to historical data, the project manager's experience in formulating estimates contributes to the project estimates' quality. It is this elusive experience factor that ensures that the project manager's early estimates developed using inexact methods are somewhat realistic and that all estimates address all the important aspects of the deliverables. The project manager's experience is an important factor in the project's success as it moves into the implementation stages and as the project team focuses on the challenges of optimizing the inevitable changes in cost, schedule, and scope.

During the inception phase of the project, very little project-specific information is available and, therefore, the estimate is not very accurate (see Figure 4-1). Part of the reason for the estimate's inaccuracy is that the probability of occurrence of undesirable project events is very high during the early stages of the project (see Figure 4-2). However, the consequences of

FIGURE 4-1 Knowledge of Details

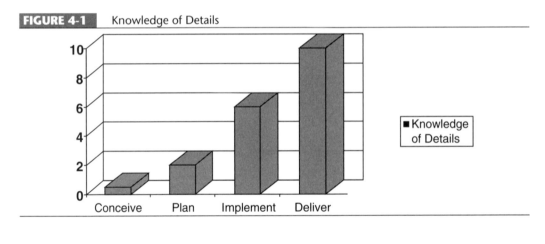

FIGURE 4-2 Uncertainties and Risks

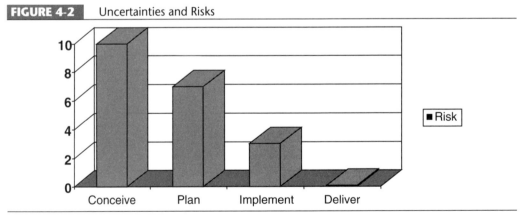

modifying project objectives are not significant because the effort spent up to that point on project design and implementation is very small (see Figures 4-3 and 4-4). Therefore, it would be ideal, although not realistic, if all the project information were available when the early estimates are made, and if no changes were made to the scope beyond this point in the project.

Considering that the likelihood of changes occurring in the project scope and environment at later stages of the project life is very high, it is necessary to note the significant financial consequences of making midstream changes to the project direction. Sometimes, these scope clarifications and/or changes make the original estimate seem highly inaccurate. It is against this backdrop and with sensitivity to the real possibility of a myriad of changes that the

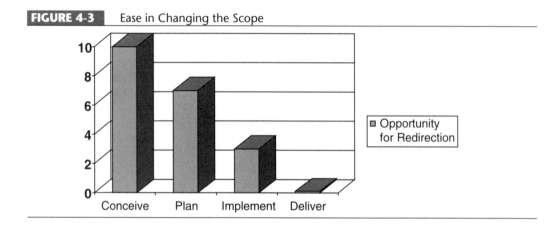

FIGURE 4-3   Ease in Changing the Scope

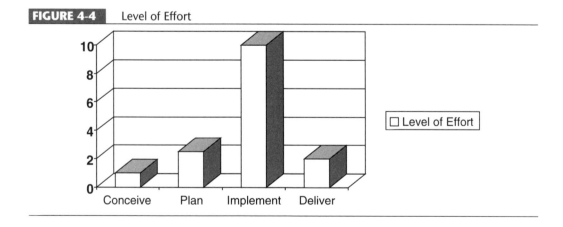

FIGURE 4-4   Level of Effort

project manager must develop rough estimates during the formative stages of the project.

Early estimates are, by their very nature, based on sketchy data and therefore extremely inaccurate. By comparison, estimates performed late in the development cycle are based on more comprehensive data. In other words, even though early estimates are inaccurate and difficult to make, they become the basis for project comparison and developing guidelines for the final project funding. Given that the project manager will make the estimate as accurate as possible considering the data available, the project stakeholders should keep the limitations of early estimates in mind when selecting projects based on these estimates, as well as during the cost management process.

Detailed and accurate estimates require substantial definitive information about the project and they also require a relatively large block of time and effort for the estimating task. Therefore, one needs to strike a balance among the time spent on estimating, the accuracy of the results, and the degree of accuracy required by the stakeholders at the point in the project life.

Estimate models compute the values of a set of dependent outputs as a function of the values of a set of independent inputs. The timing of the estimate affects how much information is available and to what degree the information is reliable. Regardless of insufficient data in the early stages, a preliminary estimate is necessary for making project decisions. This early estimate has to be made before project objectives are clarified, before project scope is defined, before requirements are fully spelled out, before the functions are clearly defined, and before the system architecture has been formulated.

During the early stages of the project and in the absence of extensive and detailed project information, project managers use a variety of tools and techniques in formulating the project estimate. These tools and techniques are usually based on models that have proven to be successful during the previous estimating efforts in this project or in other projects. These models use mathematical expressions, from the very simple to the very complex, and/or a multitude of assumptions, to estimate the cost, duration, and resource demands of one single activity, an assembly, or the entire project as a function of one or more input variables.

The techniques used by project managers for making preliminary project estimates include analogous, parametric, modular, ratio, and range estimating. The selection of the technique depends on organizational policies, the project manager's experience, and the amount of information available at the time of the estimate.

Normally, estimate models are very easy to use and they provide a quick prediction of the cost of the project, although the accuracy is not very high, particularly if the model is based on generic historical data rather than discipline-specific historical data. Therefore, any amount of effort that is spent on customizing the model to a specific project environment within an industry will have significant rewards in terms of increased accuracy and reliability of the model. As previously mentioned, the success of development and use of estimating models is highly dependent not only on the project managers' experience and competency, but also on reliable historical information.

Models used for software and systems development projects use some or all of the following data in arriving at the rough estimate: system complexity, system size, manpower skill, resource availability, specificity of project objectives, clarity of requirements, operating system features, environmental characteristics, and the extent of new technologies involved in the project. Likewise, models used for construction and industrial projects use the following data in the process of predicting project cost and duration: industry and project type, capacity and quantity, external and usable size, overall weight, project location, and the extent to which novel materials, tools, and techniques are required for the project.

Formalizing when and how cost estimates should be performed depends on the type of the project, the prevailing organizational procedures, and the degree to which the organization is concerned with project cost and overruns. Ideally, intermediate cost estimates should be performed several times during the project life, and not necessarily at budget authorization milestones. Frequent enhancement of the estimate, through regular reviews of all the cost components, improves the accuracy of the estimate. It also provides substantial historical data for refinement and enhancement of the estimating models of future projects.

ACCURACY

Depending on when the estimate is prepared and the availability of the amount and quality of historical data, the spectrum of estimates ranges from the very rough to the very detailed. An estimate can be viewed as simply a prediction of the final values of project cost and duration once the project is fully implemented. Thus, the expression of accuracy of the estimate is related to the expression of the probability that project's actual cost will match this prediction.[1,2]

As a general rule, if all the project information is available—usually toward the latter stages of the project—the accuracy of the estimate is approximately 3 percent. Therefore, the actual value may be from 97 percent to 103 percent of the estimate. Experience in construction and industrial projects has shown that, due to monitoring and reporting inaccuracies, even the estimates that are prepared late in project life are not expected to be more accurate than 3 percent or 4 percent. On the other end of the spectrum, if very little information is available, the accuracy may degrade to 233 percent. In other words, the actual value of the cost of the project might range from 33 percent to 333 percent of the estimate.

Looking at some completed projects in construction and in system development, the cost overrun can be even higher than 230 percent. Notwithstanding, it is generally accepted that estimates with little project-specific historical data developed during the inception process will be accurate to an order of magnitude; i.e., the final cost will range from 30 percent to 330 percent of the initial conceptual estimate. If sufficient project-specific historical data are available and the project manager has ample experience in this area, then he or she will be able to determine the realistic accuracy of the conceptual estimate, regardless of whether the accuracy is better or worse than an order of magnitude. The key is that if the project manager is experienced and informed about the current or previous projects, the estimates are more useful to the stakeholders.

For purposes of convenience and standardization in communication, organizations assign specific names for estimates at discrete points in the project lifecycle. The most common categorizations of estimates for external and internal projects are the following:

- Conceptual
- Order of magnitude
- Feasibility
- Preliminary
- Final
- Capital cost
- Appropriation.

The important thing to remember is that not all organizations use all these titles. Some organizations may use a subset of these to identify the estimates prepared for their projects. It is also possible that some organizations use titles that are not on this list. It is safe to assign degrees of accuracy to each of these names in internal communications, although not all organizations attribute the same characteristics and accuracies to specific estimate labels. For example, organizational procedures may specify that if an estimate is labeled as preliminary, then it will be expected to have an accuracy of 30 percent. However, for the purposes of consistency and communicating across wider administrative boundaries, sometimes organizations adopt titles, and their associated accuracies, that are recommended by professional societies such as the Association for the Advancement of Cost Engineering and the Project Management Institute.

The accuracy of the estimate, regardless of what it is called, is determined by the nature and accuracy of the historical data, just as the estimating technique formulated by the project manager depends on his or her competence in preparing it. These organizations prescribe that, as a general rule, the accuracy of the first formalized and published estimate should be better than -40 percent and +100 percent. The implication is that the estimator should be reasonably certain that the final actual cost of a project estimated at $100 should be between $60 and $200.

To use the WBS as a base of reference with very little project information available, only level zero of the WBS, which is the total project, will be estimated using any of the models described here. Once more information becomes available, individual level one elements will be estimated again using these models. The project estimate will then be the summary of level one elements, and can be expected to be more accurate. Level two items of the WBS are defined and estimated as additional information is available. Finally, once the project has been divided into its smallest units and planned at the lowest level of WBS, the lowest level units are then estimated using experience or appropriate models (see Figure 4-5). Consequently, these

FIGURE 4-5   Choice of the Model

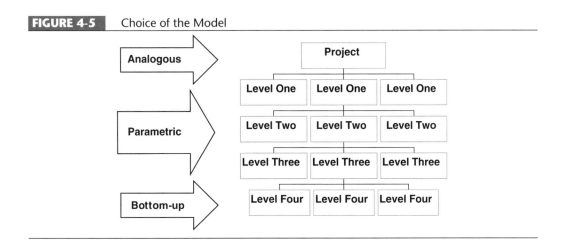

estimates are rolled up to level one items and to the total project estimate to determine the project's cost and duration.

Although simple models are inaccurate estimating tools for the total project if applied only at level zero, these models are frequently used, implicitly or explicitly, for estimating the lowest level elements even during the advanced stages of the project. If no calculation biases are built into the estimating structure, and if the WBS has a large number of lowest level elements, the repetition and the rollup process balance the inaccuracies of the models by which the lower level elements estimates were prepared.

PARAMETRIC ESTIMATING

The terms *modular estimating* and *parametric estimating* have been used to refer to two estimating models that are essentially very similar in usage, principle, and underlying structures, but have been used in different industries and, therefore, have different names. After describing the similarities and differences between these two techniques, we will use the term parametric estimating to refer to both of these techniques collectively.

Modular Estimating

Modular estimating is normally used for projects that have physical deliverables, such as refineries, power stations, office buildings, or manufacturing plants. Using this approach, the facility is characterized by indices describing the quantity and size of several key components such as power rating and number of pumps, physical size of pumps and turbines, size of the plant floor, capacity, and number of cranes. The modular model then uses historical data and predictive formulas developed for the modules' characteristics to estimate the project's cost, duration, and the amount of necessary resources. Modular estimating is used primarily in construction, process, and manufacturing projects (see Figure 4-6).

FIGURE 4-6 Modular and Parametric Models

- Physical Characteristics
  - Flow Capacity
  - Storage Capacity
  - Number of Equipment
  - Size of Equipment
- Performance Attributes
  - Speed
  - Accuracy
  - Error Tolerance
  - Reliability
  - Friendliness

Parametric Model

Similar to the modular model, the *parametric model* uses historical data as the basis of the model's predictive features. However, the characteristics that are input into the process are primarily based on performance indicators such as speed, accuracy, tolerance, reliability, friendliness, error rate, and complexity of the environment of the deliverables. Parametric estimating is used primarily in software development and system development projects. The output of parametric models includes the cost of major phases, duration of project major phases, total project cost, and resource requirements.

Parametric models calculate the dependent variables of cost and duration based on one or more independent variables. These independent variables are quantitative indices of performance and/or physical attributes. More sophisticated models provide a multitude of levels of estimates. If, during the early stages, a small array of data regarding the project is available, a rough estimate is provided. However, if a large array of project data is available later in the project's life, more accurate estimates are calculated using the same model.

A parametric model, for a construction or process project, would use the data provided by the user on any or all of the following characteristics: project type, frame material, exterior material, ground conditions, desired floor space, and roof type. Then, using the general relationships developed between these input and output variables, the model provides an estimate of some or all of the output variables. The *output variables* include cost of the design process, cost of the structure, size of major equipment, optimum size of construction crew, size of the parking lot, duration of structure construction, duration of equipment installation, and overall project duration (see Figure 4-7).

FIGURE 4-7	Construction and Industrial Projects
• Input	• Output
– Project Type	– Design Cost
– Frame Material	– Structure Cost
– Exterior Material	– Equipment Cost
– Roof Type	– Crew Size
– Ground Conditions	– Labor Cost
– Desired Floor Space	– Phase Duration
– Equipment Type	– Project Duration

Input variables for a parametric estimate for a software development project include desired reliability, database size, complexity of technology, size of the deliverable, lines of code, pages of web site, number of database records, queries per second, maximum error rate, and function points. The function points index is determined from a weighted summation of user requirements in the areas of inputs, outputs, logic files, inquiries, and interfaces. Other inputs include indicators of project environment and quantified or semi-specific project team characteristics such as skill level, physical location, and administrative affiliation. The output variables include resources needed for requirement analysis, system design, system coding, testing, integration, documentation, and system transition. The output variables also include cost and duration of these project elements, as well as for the entire project (see Figure 4-8).

Parametric estimate models are refined and fine-tuned for specific projects within specific industries. Many organizations have developed proprietarily parametric models for projects of their own specialty. Depending on the organizational environment and on the nature of targeted projects, these models use different statistically derived algorithms, which in turn would use different sets of input and output data in calculating the output variables based on the input variables. These models are, or should be, regularly evaluated, validated, calibrated, and customized for accuracy and appropriateness. The estimates of cost and duration developed by the parametric model usually establish a preliminary budget for the project that will compare its financial desirability with other projects of the enterprise.

The utility of parametric estimates is dramatic if the parametric estimate process is used to develop several estimates for alternate configurations of

FIGURE 4-8	Systems Development Projects	
• Input		• Output
– Reliability		– Analysis Cost
– Database Size		– Implementation Cost
– Project Complexity		– Transition Cost
– Error Rate		– Testing Cost
– Number of Querries		– Labor Cost
– Function Points		– Phase Duration
– Labor Skills		– Project Duration

the same potential project. However, it would be extremely dangerous to use the results of a parametric model to develop definitive budgets, unless the organization is progressive enough to allow major budget modifications as the estimate matures throughout the life of the project.

ANALOGOUS ESTIMATING

Analogous techniques are the simplest forms of estimating. *Analogous estimating* refers to the estimating process where, in the project manager's opinion, there is significant similarity between the proposed project and those projects contained in the historical database. Analogous models tend to be less complex, easier to use, and more inexact than parametric models. Analogous models are normally used for early estimates that are called order of magnitude, conceptual, or ballpark estimates. These early estimates are used to formulate rough estimates for various options and to determine the relative viability of a project in the process of screening alternate projects. Since the purpose of analogous models is to develop order of magnitude estimates based on scarce information, the project manager might make several assumptions about some of the project's environmental or functional characteristics, such as design attributes, systems engineering process, implementation techniques, and resource availability.

Analogous techniques are used to estimate project costs by comparing the proposed project with similar projects for which historical information is available. It is important when developing the analogous estimate that the project manager uses the values of as many of the following deliverable indices as available: type, functions, requirements, design characteristics, capacity, size, location, cost constraints, and quality expectations. Here again, the project manager's experience will be the deciding factor in judging the proposed project to be similar to those in the database and/or those that have formed the basis of the customized model.

Since the analogous estimating technique is based on actual experience, some software project managers contend that analogous estimating has limited use because, in many instances, no truly similar project exists in the project historical database and system development projects have no true historical precedents. These concerns will likely subside as more informed project managers collect and refine historical project data on software project languages, development methodologies, resource utilization, and complexity of system development projects.

When the project is in its inception phases, only a small amount of information is available about the specifics of the project; however, an estimate is necessary to decide on the project's viability and the profitability of the resulting product. It bears repeating that, even though an estimate is needed at that juncture, those who use the estimate must be made aware of its inaccuracies.

The analogous estimate tools described here are ratio estimating, the three-quarters rule, the square root rule, and the two-thirds rule. The significance of the structure of these models is that these rules were devised before the days of personal computers, and the numbers that they refer to make manual computations more straightforward. Notwithstanding, in the absence of extensive historical data for a specific project, these basic models provide a good first approximation for the estimate of project cost and duration. If these models are customized, the accuracy and reliability of the results will be substantially higher. Therefore, it is exceptionally useful for the project manager to keep detailed records of the ongoing project's performance. Such performance data facilitate developing appropriate exponents or ratios for estimating forthcoming projects in that specific industry or even in a specific organization within that industry.

Until the full complement of project details for individual elements of the WBS are available, the project manager provides a conceptual estimate of the total project based on minimal project-specific information. With expanded information, the project manager will develop conceptual estimates of the items at the higher levels of the WBS, e.g., levels one and two. Then, as additional information becomes available, lower level items can be estimated, making the project estimate more accurate, complete, and definitive. The key is that using a WBS as the base of reference, the estimates are not new estimates; they are simply enhancements of the original estimate. Therefore, any variances can be explained and defended more logically and rationally.

Ratio Estimating

The *equipment ratio*, or *capacity factor*, technique of estimating is one of the more basic forms of estimating in construction, industrial, and process projects. The premise of this technique is that there is a linear relationship between the cost and duration of the project and one or more of the basic features of the proposed project. The basic features in this process are related to either physical attributes or performance characteristics. The so-called ratios or factors are refined from personal experience, company files, or published industry-specific data. Although ratio estimating is deceptively simple, given an appropriate base of historical data, it is a very powerful tool in developing quick estimates for prospective projects.

For example, experience has shown that the cost of major turbines and generators in a power generation plant is nearly 30 percent of the total cost of the plant. Another example is that of a construction project where the total cost of the project is twice that of the materials and embedded equipment. Other examples include: the cost of a high-level design of a systems development project is nearly 30 percent of the total project's cost, only 20 percent of the systems project cost and effort is spent in coding, 75 percent of the cost of a systems development project is labor, or the cost of a facility's engineering design is nearly 8 percent of the project's total budget.[1-4] Further, there have been extensive efforts in developing a relationship between the estimated lines of code and the total cost of a systems development project, even though this ratio is highly environment-specific.

The Three-Quarters Rule

The *three-quarters rule* provides a simple method of developing the estimate for the total cost of a proposed project by comparing the capacity of the existing and proposed deliverable. The capacity index can be the size, speed, complexity, or accuracy of the deliverable in question. The decision of which one of these indices to use for the rough estimate depends on the objectives of the project, on whatever information is available when the estimate is made, and finally, on the experience of the project manager. Given that the relationship between any two facets of the project and the total cost may not follow the same pattern, two different size/capacity indices might produce different estimates for the new project. Therefore, for best results, as many indices as possible should be used in determining the estimate. Then, by simple averaging, or by weighted averaging, of these individual estimates, a more tempered project estimate will be obtained.

This estimating rule is a slightly more sophisticated version of the ratio estimating technique, where there is an assumed equality between the ratios and the exponents of equipment sizes and overall project costs. The three-quarters rule, aptly named, is based on the following formula:

Analogous Estimating Rules of Thumb

- Three-Quarters Rule
  $C_p = C_e (S_p/S_e)^{.75}$

- Square Root Rule
  $T_p = T_e (C_p/C_e)^{.5}$

- Two-Thirds Rule
  $T_p = T_e (N_p/N_e)^{.66}$

Variables $T_p\, T_e$ = Project Duration
      $C_p\, C_e$ = Cost
      $S_p\, S_e$ = Size or Capabity
      $N_p\, N_e$ = Concurrent Subsystems

The premise of this rule is that if the ratio of the capacities, or sizes, of the proposed and current projects is raised to the power of ¾, it will provide an indicator of the ratio of the cost of the two projects. This technique can be used to make extrapolations or interpolations either graphically or computationally and both can be performed with the use of spreadsheet software. The following display shows the computational application of this rule to predict the cost of houses with two, five, or six bedrooms, where the project manager has only the cost for a three-bedroom house.

The Three-Quarters Rule
Estimate Cost of a House Based on the Number of Bedrooms

Current House: 3 Bedrooms, $37,500
Proposed House: 5 Bedrooms

(Cost of New Facility)/(37500) = ((5)/(3))**(3/4)
Cost of a Five Bedroom House = $55,007

Cost of a Six Bedroom House = $63,067
Cost of a Two Bedroom House = $27,667

Figure 4-9 shows a graphic application of the same example. If one uses a log-log scale when using the graphic application of this method, the model

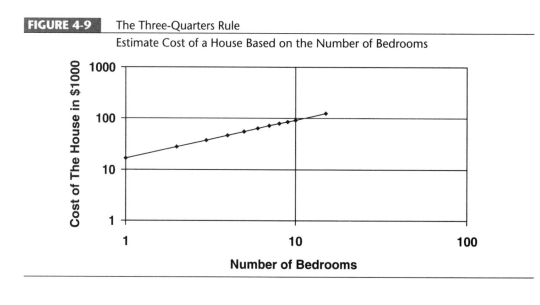

FIGURE 4-9 The Three-Quarters Rule

Estimate Cost of a House Based on the Number of Bedrooms

data will be displayed in a straight line, making visual interpolation very easy. Figure 4-10 shows the application of this technique to the cost of apartment complexes based on the number of units in each complex.

If enough industry-specific or organization-specific data are available, this technique can be refined to reflect the specifics of that industry in conjunction with that particular capacity index used for extrapolation. Then, for future estimates, a customized variation of this technique will be used to arrive at more accurate conceptual estimates. This modification is referred to as the modified three-quarters rule. Thus, using the existing data, an exponent other than ¾ will be suggested for this particular project environment. Again, it is important to note that the cost exponent will be different for different capacity indices and, therefore, a different exponent needs to be developed for each capacity index. Then the results can be combined to formulate a more refined estimate.

The following modified three-quarters rule shows how an exponent of .96 was obtained for a particular class of construction projects. It is an important point that computation and recording of the value of the exponents is necessary only in the computational method. If the graphic method is used, it is not necessary to be aware of the value of the exponent;

FIGURE 4-10   The Three-Quarters Rule

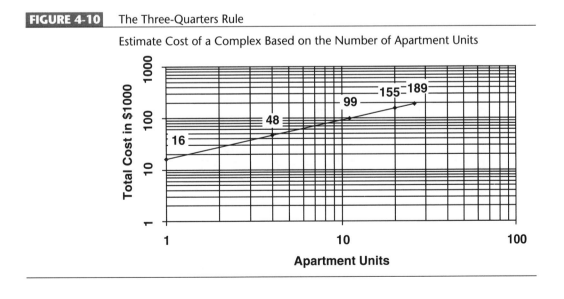

using a straight-line extrapolation or interpolation, the cost of the proposed project can be determined.

The Modified Three-Quarters Rule
Estimate Cost of a House Based on the Number of Bedrooms

Current Facility: 3 Bedroom House, $70,000
Current Facility: 4 Bedroom House, $90,000

Proposed House: 6 Bedroom House?

$(90/70) = ((4/3)**?)$ $? = 0.96$

$(\text{Cost of New Facility})/(70,000) = ((6)/(3))**(.96)$

Cost of New Facility = $128,000

Figure 4-11 shows a graphic application of this technique without any specific reference to the value of the exponent. Using any two data points, the straight line defining the model can be defined, based on which future estimates can be made very quickly. Figure 4-12 shows the application of this model to develop a model to estimate the cost of airport expansions.[5] This model used the cost of completed airports, such as Newark, JFK, and Hartsfield, to develop a conceptual estimate for the total cost of the Denver Airport. The index that was used for comparison was the terminal's size in square feet.

FIGURE 4-11 Modified Three-Quarters Rule
Estimate Cost of a House Based on the Number of Bedrooms

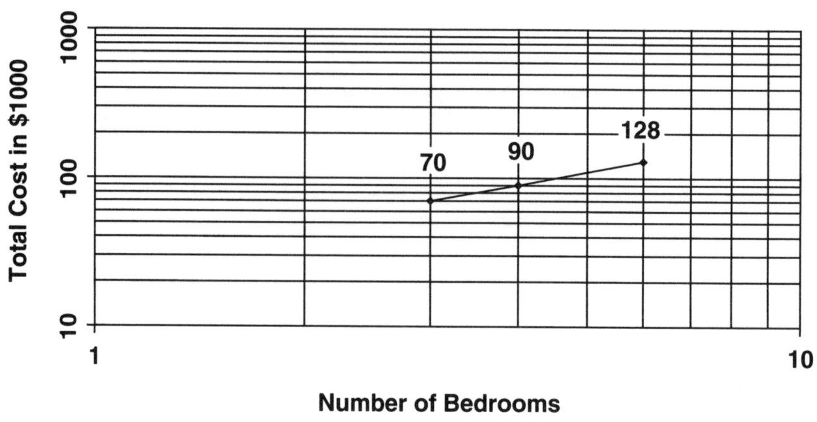

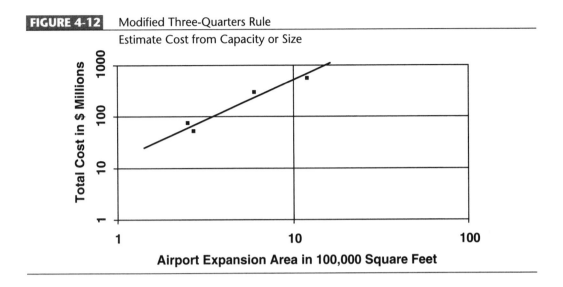

FIGURE 4-12   Modified Three-Quarters Rule

Estimate Cost from Capacity or Size

The Square Root Rule

The *square root technique* allows the project manager to predict the duration of a proposed project on the basis of comparing the costs of existing and proposed projects. The square root rule, also aptly named, is based on the formula shown earlier in the chapter in the section on the three-quarters rule. The premise of this rule is that the square root of the ratio of the costs of the proposed and current projects provides an indicator of the ratio of the duration of the two projects.

The estimate below and the graph in Figure 4-13 show the application of the computational mode of this technique to determine the cost and construction duration of a 340-room dormitory when the only pieces of information available are the cost and duration of construction of 200-room dormitory. Figure 4-14 shows the graphic representation of a model developed from historical highway construction data.

The Square Root Rule
For a Dormitory—Estimate Duration from Cost

Current Facility: 200 Rooms, 12 Months, $10.4 Million

Proposed Facility: 340 Rooms, $14.8 Million

(Duration for New Facility)/(12) = ((14.8)/(10.4))**(1/2)

Duration for New Facility = 14.3 Months

FIGURE 4-13 The Square Root Rule

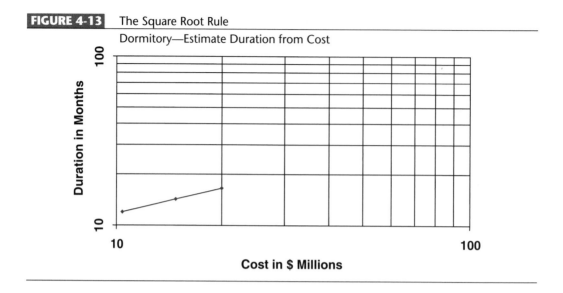

Dormitory—Estimate Duration from Cost

Using existing data from similar projects, an industry-specific exponent can be developed. This modification can be referred to as the modified square root technique. The estimate on the next page and the graph in Figure 4-15 show the computational and graphic development of the exponent for process

FIGURE 4-14 The Square Root Rule

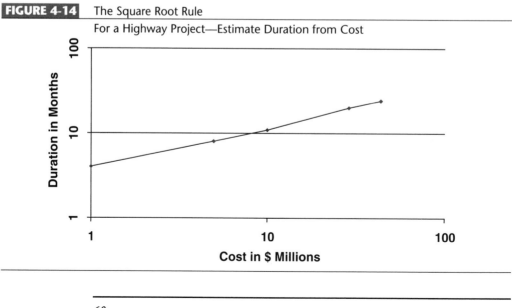

For a Highway Project—Estimate Duration from Cost

| FIGURE 4-15 | The Modified Square Root Rule |

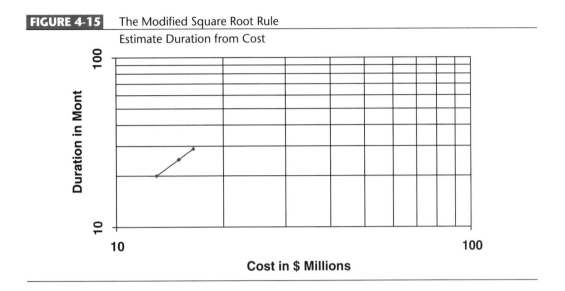

Estimate Duration from Cost

plants on the basis of existing projects. The graphic or the computational method then can be used for future projects.

The Modified Square Root Rule
Estimate Duration from Cost

Current Facility: 13 Months, $20 Million
Current Facility: 15 Months, $25 Million

$(15/(13)) = ((25)/(20))^{**}(?) ? = 0.641$

Proposed Facility: $29 Million

(Duration of Proposed Facility)/(15) = $(29/25)^{**}.641$

Duration of Proposed Facility = 16.5 Months

Figure 4-16 shows the graphic application of this technique to the airport expansion data mentioned in the previous section.

The Two-Thirds Rule

The *two-thirds technique* will allow the project manager to sharpen the duration estimate of a proposed project if the project contains several concurrent and similar activities. This adjustment is intended to refine the estimates of the project's duration when the same project personnel are assigned to

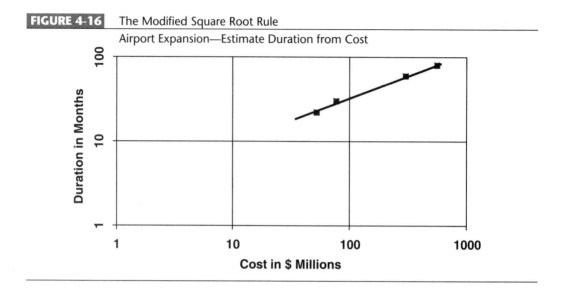

FIGURE 4-16 The Modified Square Root Rule

Airport Expansion—Estimate Duration from Cost

similar tasks within the project or within a unified program but to similar projects. The two-thirds rule is based on the formula that is shown earlier in the chapter in the section on the three-quarters rule. The premise of this rule is that if the ratio of the number of concurrent subsystems is raised to the power of 2/3, it will provide an indicator of the ratio of the duration of the two projects. Examples include building several apartment complexes at the same time, designing several web pages at the same time, building several specialty airplanes at the same time, installing several servers at the same time, or pulling several sets of fiber optics cables during the same time frame.

Although this model addresses only the duration of the project, the presumption is that the multiple concurrent systems will affect the cost of the project in the same manner as they affect the duration. Finally, as in previous models, a sufficient amount of historical data will allow customization of the exponent of this model to specific project environments.

RANGE ESTIMATING

Another approach to increasing the reliability of the early estimates, know as *range estimating*, is to provide not just one estimate for the cost of an element but rather define the range of possible values for the cost of a specific element. This concept was the foundation of the PERT technique by which probabilistic project duration is obtained through the use of multiple durations defined for individual activity durations. Then, in addition to the deterministic project duration defined by the estimator's prediction, a range of probable and likely duration values is computed.

Range estimating uses the same statistical fundamentals in estimating total project cost based on probabilistic elemental costs. Thus, in addition to providing one number as the total possible cost of an element of the WBS, which reflects the opinion of the project manager, two other values are also provided. One is the most pessimistic estimate and the other is the most optimistic estimate. Using these three values, the most likely cost for the element or the project can be determined. Equally useful, if this three-value set is available for all the elements of a fully developed WBS, a random number generation tool can be used to develop a likely cost for the project. Additionally, this three-number set will allow development of probability distributions for the project cost, and a probable cost for the project based on random selection of elemental estimates.

In many cases, the most likely values derived from the application of this statistical method are higher than the deterministic values derived from the summation of single estimate values provided by the project manager. This revelation highlights the premise that project managers and project estimators are fundamentally optimistic, and therefore, they tend to underestimate the cost and duration of a project.

Figure 4-17 shows the calculation of elemental values of the most likely costs based on the three values provided by the project manager. If the three values provided by the project manager are 5, 8, and 35, the most likely estimate for that element, as provided by this model, is 12. The net result of using this model is that the estimate is steered toward the mean of the optimistic and pessimistic values, primarily because the deterministic value is dangerously close to the most optimistic value.

FIGURE 4-17   Range Estimating

- Elements
  - Optimistic Time, TO
  - Most Likely Time, TM
  - Pessimistic Time, TP
- Calculate Expected Time For Each Activity
  - TE = (TO + 4TM + TP) / 6
  - Standard Deviation = (TP-TO) / 6

On the other hand, if the three estimates provided by the project manager are 5, 20, and 35, the most likely value predicted by this model will be 20; note that 20 is the estimate that was considered most likely by the project manager also. The point is not that every deterministic estimate should be the mean of optimistic and pessimistic values, but that one needs to be careful not to be overly optimistic in estimating every aspect of the project. Finally, although range estimating can be used to fully develop WBSs, the use of range estimating is far more valuable when the WBS elements have not been fully defined beyond the first and second levels, and when the cost of these elements is at the order-of-magnitude accuracy.

EXPERT JUDGMENT

Many semi-experienced project managers depend on more experienced project managers and the experts of the field to validate the conceptual estimates of a project, regardless of how the estimate was prepared. Even experienced project managers often consult with their peers in order to fine-tune what they believe is a reasonable estimate. The *expert judgment* technique involves consulting one or more experts to validate the estimate of the proposed project against the experience and understanding of the experts, who will consider the details of project complexities and characteristics in tempering the estimate or concurring with it.

Using an expert judgment opinion is somewhat akin to identifying and using the results of a parametric technique of personal nature, which is based on intuition, experience, and not-yet-articulated indices. Nonetheless, until these unspoken extrapolation techniques are formalized, expert judgment will remain one of the more reliable sources for checking the realism of the estimates, particularly in software and systems development projects.

NORMALIZATION

Once the cost and duration of a proposed project have been predicted from historical data, the resulting values need to be adjusted and normalized in the light of time and location differences between the proposed project and those that formed the basis for the model (see Figure 4-18).

The term *time* refers to the year in which the existing project was completed. Comparison between the delivery dates would provide the basis to adjust the estimate based on the inflation rate or the time value of money. The term *location adjustment* would account for the differences in salaries and in cost of materials in different locations. For example, if the database contains information from projects that have been performed in the United

FIGURE 4-18   Sample Computations

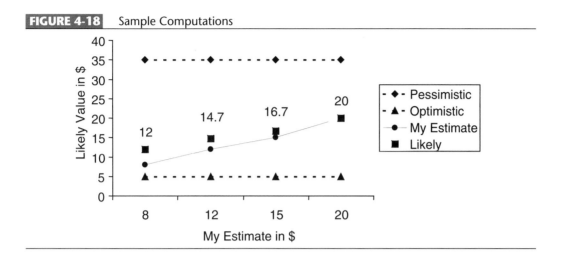

States, and if the proposed project is to be performed in China or Italy, differences in locality-based cost factors must be considered when finalizing the estimate for project cost. This adjustment is conducted by a simple ratio adjustment. For example, once the time-adjusted estimate of a project is determined, then that estimate will be adjusted again by a factor of, say, 1.12, in order to account for project cost differences in those two locations. The third adjustment factor, *capacity*, which is shown in Figure 4–19, has been covered in detail earlier in this chapter.

FIGURE 4-19   Analogous Estimate

- It is usually the very first estimate conducted for the project
- It uses the available information to arrive at the estimate
- Generally, the available information is extrapolated and adjusted in the light of
  - Time: the year in which the project was completed
  - Location: the location of the current/proposed project
  - Capacity: size or capacity comparison between the current and proposed project

Estimating models are the tools that leverage the estimator's experience and the admittedly sparse project data in developing a prediction for the final cost of the project. This leveraging becomes more effective and almost approaches a science when the tool is modified and sharpened with historical data pertaining to the area of the project. Given that early estimates have a profound effect on whether the project gets initiated, estimating models tend to take on a pivotal role in project selection, as well as in the development of the planning-phase estimates of the project. Conceptually, any estimating model can be used to predict the cost of projects in any industry, although estimating professionals in different industries have gravitated to specific models for the purpose of developing project estimates.

NOTES

1. Anonymous, *Parametric Estimating Handbook*, 2nd ed. (Washington, DC: US Department of Defense, 1999).
2. Anonymous, *RS Means Construction Reference Books* (Kingston, MA: RS Means Company, 2000).
3. Anonymous, *Skills and Knowledge of Cost Engineering*, 4th Ed. (Morgantown, WV: AACE, 1999).
4. M.R. Vigder and A.W. Kark, *Software Cost Estimation and Control* (Ottawa, Ontario, Canada: National Research Council of Canada, February 1994).
5. D.S. Remer and C. Wong, Cost Scale UP Factors for Airport Construction, *Cost Engineering* 38, no.2 (February 1996): 24-26.

CHAPTER 5

Progress Monitoring

Monitoring project performance is essential to keep the project manager informed of the status of the deliverable. Data collected during the progress monitoring process are crucial in managing the issues and circumstances brought on by the project's inevitable changes. The focus and emphasis of project progress monitoring is fundamentally different from traditional cost accounting. *Cost accounting* deals with issues involved in reporting the expenses to the correct components of the established budget for the cost centers and codes of account. While cost accounting is focused on collecting accurate actual cost information with specific attention to the elements of the code of accounts, *project progress monitoring* focuses on areas of resource expenditure as delineated by the WBS.

There is no question that accurate collection of cost information should be part of the data collected and/or computed by a project monitoring system. However, cost is not the primary concern of the data collection, but rather the deliverable-specific resource expenditure data are the area of concern.

The observed variances in resource expenditure and cost are used to identify trends that will in turn be used to make midcourse adjustments to project plans. The reliance on RBS and WBS, provided by a formalized progress monitoring system, allows project managers to compile meaningful historical data that will be useful in managing the changes in the texture of the current project, while providing useful historical data for streamlining the estimating and managing of future projects.

In the same vein that the accuracy and efficiency of the project estimate depend on data collected from previous experiences in similar projects, a formalized monitoring system will be very useful in collecting historical data for cost estimating models and general organizational memory, which will benefit the effectiveness of future projects. In essence, although the progress monitoring system benefits the project at-hand significantly, it has far-reaching benefits for organizational project management effectiveness.

Progress monitoring is most successful when it is formalized and fully embedded into the organizational procedures for managing projects. Therefore, progress monitoring procedures should be part of the organizational project management culture rather than narrowly focused on the project at-hand.

The progress monitoring system should be formulated and implemented such that it will not negatively impact the efficiency, creativity, innovation, and morale of the technical personnel of the project team. It must be a facilitative tool that informs the team members of their individual assignments, reminds them of forthcoming events, and warns them if there are significant variances. Additionally, the progress monitoring system centrally stores data for forecasting and for future customization of estimating models.

The function of a progress monitoring system is to keep the project team informed of the progress of their task and apprised of progress in attaining overall objectives by all the team members. As such, the progress monitoring system should be regarded as nothing other than a valuable aid. Unfortunately, in many creativity-based and highly specialized projects, the project team might regard progress reporting as cumbersome, intrusive, and a signal that senior management does not trust the project team. Project managers often reinforce and perpetuate these sentiments by using progress data to pressure individual task leaders to deliver products faster. Further, divisional managers with a misguided objective of efficiency and improvement use progress data to micromanage the project team, and thereby provide unwitting affirmation for the team's negative attitude toward progress monitoring measures.

In other instances, particularly in projects that involve a great deal of creativity and new technology, project team members regard progress monitoring as an affront to creativity. Ironically, a logical progress monitoring system will not impede creativity, but instead will assist the team members in understanding the cost/schedule implications of their contributions to the project, thus allowing the project professionals to concentrate on producing superior deliverables. With proper education and indoctrination, the majority of the team members and upper management will likely adopt a healthier and more appropriate view of progress monitoring.

If the organization is progressive enough to have a project management office (PMO), much of the formalization of the progress reporting process is handled as part of the charter of the PMO. Many organizations do, in fact, have a project management culture and a commitment to formalized project management, but this organizational entity is not called a PMO. Therefore, the key is that the organization must have the important organizational facets that facilitate the proper conduct of projects. The facets necessary for achieving the desired goals in project management are:

- Organizational commitment to project management principles
- A set of consistent procedures
- A battery of operational tools.

The basic foundation for a project management culture is the firm commitment to principles of project management, such as formal scope definition for every project, extensive use of the major project structures, logical cost management policies, and usable cost reporting procedures (see Figure 5-1). These principles will be reinforced with the use of enterprise guidelines and procedures necessary for project initiation, approval, mobilization, implementation, and closeout (see Figure 5-2).

Finally, the project team members must have at their disposal a set of operational tools that facilitates compliance with enterprise project management policies. These tools, which must be updated and expanded regularly to remain state-of-the-art, include data capture forms, scheduling methodologies, progress reporting forms, and software packages such as PM software, databases, spreadsheets, and presentation graphics (see Figure 5-3).

FIGURE 5-1　　Project Management Principles

- **Define Project Objective and Scope**
- **Devise Project Execution Plan**
- **Identify WBS, RBS, OBS**
- **Organize Budget and Schedule**
- **Develop Progress Reporting Schemes**
- **Formulate Analysis Criteria**
- **Establish Monitoring Guidelines**
- **Manage Unexpected Changes**

FIGURE 5-2　　Project Management Consistent Procedures

- **Project Approval**
- **Scope Development**
- **Budget Preparation and Approval**
- **Project Mobilization**
- **Progress Reporting**
- **Management of Change**
- **Collection of Historical Data**

FIGURE 5-3   Project Management Operational Tools

- **Data Capture Forms**
- **CPM and PERT Methodology**
- **Software Packages**
  - Project Management
  - Database Manipulation
  - Presentation Graphics
- **Progress Reports**
- **Progress Meetings**

The project monitoring policy and tools are not meant to be restrictive, but rather informative and facilitative. To that end, as the organization matures and as creative project teams contribute to the design and conduct of the monitoring process, the suitability, applicability, and usability of the project management tools and techniques will continually improve.

DEVELOPING A MONITORING PLAN

Normally, the vision for a new project or a new corporate initiative is approved at the higher levels of the corporate structure, including the following project stakeholders:

- President
- Divisional vice-president
- Manager of projects
- Project manager
- Senior project planner
- Project staff.

Such a vision might either emanate from the organization's upper levels or, in more enlightened organizations, be developed at the project level and presented to upper management for approval. As the implementation of this initiative is delegated to lower levels of the organization, a more detailed definition of this vision is developed.

The directive that is drafted at the chief executive officer (CEO) level may be a one-paragraph or even a one-line vision (see Figure 5-4). However, by the time this initiative is developed at the lower levels of the organization, it may involve many pages of descriptive design and hardware specifications. Using WBS terminology, level zero of the project is specified at the top levels of the organization, and the lower levels are developed, designed, and implemented by the subsequent levels of the organization's project team members.

FIGURE 5-4   Project Plans

Concept
Concept Concept
Concept Strategy Concept
Strategy Concept Plan Strategy
Plan Plan Strategy Plan Plan Strategy
Detailed Plan Detailed Plan Detailed Plan

Likewise, when the data are compiled, refined, and tabulated, it is important that the same level of detail contained in the data's refinement or analysis is also contained in the reports that are distributed. Detailed project data are exceptionally useful to the project team members, and yet overwhelming to those who are not intimately involved with the project. The best data collection and reporting systems are those that customize the level of detail to the organizational stature and involvement level of the person supplying the information or the person receiving the report.

Accordingly, project staff members should get all possible details regarding their own tasks, interdependent tasks, and the project in general. However, at the other end of the spectrum, the CEO will probably get a one- or two-line report on the status of the project's cost and schedule, and definitely not with the same frequency that the team receives reports. Naturally, if the CEO would like additional information, it can be made available (see Figure 5-5).

As noted, the data collection and reporting process must be at the appropriate level of detail for the person supplying the information and for the person receiving the report. Additionally, the data that are collected and the trends that are reported must be at a level of detail that allows detection of deviations of the actual value from the baseline project plan. Finally, the report frequency must be such that the project team can deploy corrective measures in a timely and useful manner, if the variances indicate the need for a change in the project's pace.

FIGURE 5-5   Data and Reports

Report
Report Report
Report Analyze Report
Analyze Report Capture Analyze
Capture Capture Analyze Capture Analyze
Capture Capture Capture Capture Capture Capture

The same degree of specificity used in the project's inception process for generating project definition documents must be applied to the progress reports' definition of contents and the distribution pattern. The progress monitoring procedures must specify how often the data sampling should be conducted and how often the progress reports should be issued. When developing data capture procedures, all affected parties must agree on the following:

- Who will collect the data
- Who will provide the data
- How often the data will be provided
  —Every day
  —Every Monday
  —First day of the month
  —First day of the quarter
- What is the expected tolerance of the data.

For example, if the item to be measured is the number of programs written or the volume of concrete poured, the project charter must specify whether the measurement is performed by the technical person doing the work or by the administrative staff in charge of data collection. Beyond that, specifics of the frequency of data collection must be outlined beforehand; for example, whether the data will be collected every day, each Monday, the first day of each month, or the first day of the quarter.

Those project stakeholders who receive progress reports should be fully aware of what is expected of them in response to the contents of the report. Some stakeholders will receive the report for information only and no action will be required of them. Others may receive the report for review and action. The type of action and the turnaround time must be specified as part of the project charter (see Figure 5-6). This kind of specificity will ultimately

---

FIGURE 5-6   Data and Reports

- **Frequency of Report Distribution**
  – Daily, Monday, Month, Quarter
- **Personnel Receiving the Report for Information Only**
- **Personnel Receiving the Report for Action**
  – Action Type:
    • Phone, turnaround, input sheet, meeting, memo, letter, report
  – Urgency:
    • Action expected within hours/days/weeks/months

---

introduce efficiency and expediency into the conduct of the project. With these precautions in place, the volume of a progress report will not overwhelm the recipients when their involvement in the project is minimal. Further, there will be few occasions when someone is not sure why he or she is the recipient of a progress report. More to the point, those who need to react to the project events get the correct and sufficient information to execute their duties.

Under these circumstances, project personnel know what is expected of them in terms of data needed for input into the progress reporting system. Accordingly, the project personnel have a clear picture of the volume, quality, and frequency of the reports they will receive. To increase the utility of the progress monitoring and reporting system, the collected data must be compiled and refined as part of each data collection cycle. Then, the refined data and analysis should be reported to the team in a timely manner with the level of detail useful to the recipient.

ELEMENTS OF MONITORING

The objective of a progress monitoring system is to provide formalized data capture procedures that allow development of a set of logical and rational indices by which the pace of attaining the objectives is measured. Progress is measured in the areas of cost, schedule, and scope. Baseline data may be the original baseline data, although in most cases it is a modified version of the original baseline. To clarify, the purpose of progress monitoring is not to force the project progress and its associated costs to the figures that were predefined as part of the plans and budget, but rather the purpose is to report accurate values of actual project performance indices.

The project manager might use the progress data as a basis for making adjustments to the work pace. Alternately, the project manager might conclude that it is more appropriate to draft a budget modification request. Naturally, the project manager may make an informed determination that the variances are transient or not significant, and that no major changes need to be made.

In some organizational environments, lapsed time and cost of labor are considered indications of progress. Although these indicators are good means to measure the cost incurred, they do not have a direct relationship with progress, and therefore, they can be misleading and highly inaccurate. A more rational set of progress indices includes measurements of what has been delivered and indications of the rate of resource expenditures with respect to each deliverable. The raw progress data for each activity should contain as many of the following pieces of information as possible:

- Actual start date of the activity
- Volume of deliverables
- Effort spent so far
- Hours spent so far
- Hours spent on the deliverable
- Work days elapsed
- Effort needed to finish the activity.

The raw data, by which progress will be recorded, might also include work days spent, worker days spent, total cost of labor, and total cost of materials and/or equipment. Notwithstanding, during the progress data capture activities, care must be taken to distinguish between worker days, workdays, and elapsed days.

Examples of progress indicators in construction projects are number of feet of wire pulled, cubic yards of concrete poured, and square feet of carpet installed. Examples of progress indices in systems development projects are number of screens completed, number of lines of code written, and number of machines enabled. For tasks that have a series of sequential subtasks, the achieved milestones can be a measure of progress. Examples of task milestones for a server installation project could be receive, place, connect, test, accept, and turnover.

For creativity-based tasks, where the deliverable often defies measurement and where progress is an illusive and immeasurable concept, guidelines need to be established for how to measure project progress. Depending on the organizational culture, project complexity, and the needs of the project, one of several crediting methods can be applied. For some activities, progress credit can be applied when the task is started and credit can be applied incrementally as progress is made. In other organizational environments, one must apply a binary system in which credit is applied only when the completed deliverable is received. Under this system, no credit will be applied if the deliverable has not been received, regardless of how much time and money have been spent on the task. Naturally, a variety of intermediate crediting methods can be devised to accommodate situations that do not call for either of these two extremes. A partial list of possible crediting methods is shown in Figure 5-7.

The rationale for the development and use of these crediting schemas is to provide project management data as accurately as possible with minimal

FIGURE 5-7   Progress Reporting for Nonmeasurable Activities

- **The 0%–100% Rule**
  - The team will not be credited for progress unless the deliverable is fully delivered
- **The 20%–80% Rule**
  - The team will get 20% for starting the task. Full credit will be applied upon delivery
- **The 50%–50% Rule**
  - The team will be credited for half of the deliverable upon starting and half upon delivery
- **The 30%–30%–40% Rule**
  - Not Started   Team will be credited for   0%
  - Just Started   Team will be credited for   30%
  - In Progress   Team will be credited for   60%
  - Completed   Team will be credited for   100%

intrusion into the technical facets of a particular task. Although these crediting guidelines seem imprecise—and they are in fact imprecise at the elemental level—once they are summarized across the WBS levels, the overall progress of the higher levels of WBS can be acceptably accurate.

EARNED VALUE

The calculation of earned value is a very effective tool in measuring the progress of contractors in external projects. Computation of earned value can be part of an audit activity, or it can be integrated into the progress monitoring system. The concept of earned value is generally used in the context of fixed price contracts where the objective is to calculate the amount of payment that is due to the contractor.

However, to the extent that earned value reflects the magnitude of progress, it is useful in internal projects also. It serves as an equally powerful tool in determining the rate of progress of internal projects toward achieving the project's goals.

At any point during the life of the project, the amount of progress, as indicated by the earned value of the project, can be determined by summarizing the earned value of lower level components along the WBS structure. The project's earned value can be computed by determining the percentage of earned value for each of the constituent components at the lower levels of the WBS. For both the early stages of the project and for small projects, this process involves only a few elements at the first one or two levels. For fully developed projects, the process involves a very large set of all of the project's lower level components, extending to levels four, five, and even lower, of the WBS.

The value that is earned for each WBS element is determined by summing the progress made in each of the tasks performed to deliver the WBS element at-hand. Figure 5-8 shows the procedure for establishing an earned value system for a deliverable element. The first step is the formulation of a list of values during the planning stages. Then, at the reporting milestones, it is possible to determine the progress credited to each of the constituents, using any of the crediting methods described earlier. Total earned value is the sum of the products of the value amounts and credited progress.

Figures 5-9, 5-10, and 5-11 show the development of earned value for a segment of a web site development project. Figure 5-9 shows a listing of values defined during the planning stages by the stakeholders for this project. The value list can be a compilation of the distribution of either cost or effort among the activities of the element under evaluation. The progress of the team in achieving the goals of the element in question is indicated by the total

---

FIGURE 5-8   Earned Value

- During Planing Stage of Project
  - Divide the Work into Discrete Components
  - Assign Cost to Each Component
  - Agree on Earned Value Payment
- During Execution Stage of Project
  - Determine Progress on Each Component
  - Calculate the Earned Value

FIGURE 5-9   Sample Earned Value—Web Site Development Value List

Activity Description	*Total ExpectedValue*
• Requirements	10%
• Design	20%
• Develop Modules	30%
• Test Modules	20%
• Integration Test	5%
• Document and Train	15%
• Total Deliverables	100%

| FIGURE 5-10 | Sample Earned Value—Web Site Development |

Item	*Portion Delivered*
• Requirements	100%
• Design	85%
• Develop Modules	80%
• Test Modules	10%
• Integration Test	0%
• Document & Train	0%
• Total Progress	?%

| FIGURE 5-11 | Sample Earned Value—Web Site Development |

Activity	*Total Value Expected*	*Position Delivered*	*Earned*
• Requirements	10%	100%	10%
• Design	20%	85%	17%
• Develop Modules	30%	80%	24%
• Test Modules	20%	10%	2%
• Integration Test	5%	0%	0%
• Document and Train	15%	0%	0%
• Total Earned	100%	?%	53%

earned value. This progress is determined by summing the credits earned by each of the constituent activities, toward the deliverable, as shown in Figure 5-10. Accordingly, Figure 5-11 shows a computation of the value earned for the deliverable element. The assigned progress percentages do not have to be exceptionally accurate; in fact, due to the nature of many creativity-based projects, the accuracy of the assigned progress percentages is somewhat low. Again, notwithstanding the inaccuracy at the lowest level, once the earned values are rolled up to the project level, the accuracy is acceptable if there are no overt biases in determining the elemental earned value.

Some project managers choose to use a more extensive schema for earned value. This schema is fundamentally based on four terms that are listed below. These terms, and the resulting predictive indices, are calculated and/or refreshed at the project's evaluation milestones. The terminology listed here is the original one defined in the 1970s. The shorthand notations listed in parentheses have recently been recommended by the Project Management Institute:

- BCWS, Budgeted Cost of Work Scheduled (PV)—What was planned to be done
- ACWP, Actual Cost of Work Performed (AC) —What was spent
- BCWP, Budgeted Cost of Work Performed (EV)—What was done
- Budget at Completion (BAC)—Amount budgeted for the entire project.

Then, the following series of evaluative and predictive ratios will be used to assess the current state of the project and to predict the future direction of the project:

- BCWP–ACWP =CV   Cost Variance—amount of cost overrun or underrun
- BCWP-BCWS = SV   Schedule Variance—schedule overrun or underrun in $
- BCWP/ACWP =CPI   Cost Performance Index—normalized cost overrun or underrun
- BCWP/BCWS = SPI   Schedule Performance Index—normalized schedule over/underrun
- BAC/CPI =EAC   Estimate at Completion—updated estimate of total project cost
- BAC-EAC= VAC   Variance at Completion—amount of over/underrun at delivery
- (BAC-BCWP)/CPI= ETC   Estimate to Complete—funds needed to complete the project

PRODUCTIVITY

The term *productivity* is usually associated with concepts such as:
- Spending less money
- Taking less time
- Using less effort
- Improving quality
- Creating less waste
- Reducing rework volume
- Creating more output with less input.

Productivity is affected by the characteristics of the project team, such as:
- Personal pride
- Attitude
- Competency

- Motivation to learn
- Desire to excel
- Organizational culture
- Type of contract.

The specificity of the project objectives, clarity of project plan, and availability of tools, particularly with respect to individual assignments, also affect the productivity of the team.

Productivity is also affected by the frequency of unexpected and unexplained changes to the project and the presence of a formalized scope change policy. Productivity depends on the environment created by organizational policies and procedures with respect to innovation, efficiency, and reward. Finally, experience has shown that the productivity of the contractor's team is additionally affected by the nature of the contract.

The following client factors affect productivity:
- Specificity of project objectives
- Clarity of project plan
- Availability of tools
- Frequency of scope changes
- Formalized scope change policy
- Organizational policies.

Strategies that improve the productivity of the workforce include assigning the correct specialty and correct competency level to each task. Proper assignment of labor will greatly enhance team morale, and verification of such assignment should be an integral part of project progress monitoring.

Sometimes, particularly in projects that involve lengthy or highly repeatable tasks, productivity is expressed by a *learning curve*. The premise in the concept of a learning curve is that if a task is performed repeatedly, it will take less time to perform that particular task as more iterations are performed. As an example, designing a web page might take 120 minutes for someone who is doing it for the first time. But, as the same person designs similar pages, each repetition will take a little less time so that the 30th page can be done in, for example, 100 minutes. The extent to which this improvement occurs is determined from plotting task time versus the number of repetitions, otherwise known as the learning curve.

Since the learning curve is usually plotted on a log-log scale, a line on that scale will characterize the learning curve. Figure 5-12 shows three separate lines (curves) indicating the rate of productivity improvement for three different operations. This graph shows that after 32 repetitions, one operation gains a 10 percent reduction in performance time while another

FIGURE 5-12 Learning Curves

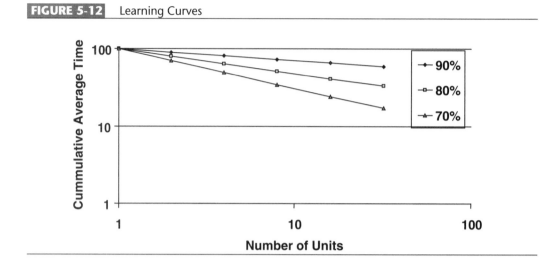

gains a 30 percent reduction in performance time. For lengthy projects that include highly repetitive tasks, the effect of the learning curve on project cost and duration performance should be considered.

The project manager's effectiveness in dealing with the implementation issues of the project depends heavily on having timely and accurate data that describe the progress of crafting, building, and creating the various components of the project. The objective of a good monitoring system is to keep the project manager informed of the expenditures and achievements that are associated with the project deliverable. These tasks must be conducted as quickly, accurately, and regularly as possible. The data to be collected will focus on attributes of the resources, the amount of resources, and the project elements on which these resources were spent. Additionally, a logical and proactive monitoring system will highlight the rate of attainment of elemental objectives, particularly in comparison with the anticipated rate of achieving the goals and objectives.

CHAPTER 6

Cost Management

C*ost management* is the process used to minimize the cost of the project while maintaining acceptable levels of quality as well as the scope of the deliverables for the duration of the project. Project information that forms the basis of a progress monitoring and cost management system includes a detailed description of client objectives, project requirements, quality expectations, resource constraints, funding structure, acceptance test details, administrative milestones, and the anticipated delivery date.

The cost management process is most effective when it is formalized and integrated with the enterprise's project management policies and procedures. A formalized cost management process ensures that all project personnel in all projects follow a specific set of established procedures. A formal management structure has the added advantage of keeping all project stakeholders involved in, or at least informed of, the performance status of the project, thereby contributing to team spirit and good morale.

The objectives of the cost management process are to track progress, compare actual values to planned values, analyze the impact of variances, and make adjustments in light of these variances. Progress data from the current project are interpreted in the light of historical data from previous projects and/or benchmarking data from other projects within the same industry. These interpretations must be repeated or refreshed on a regular basis, particularly as part of the inevitable changes throughout the life of the project. The impact of each change must be evaluated in terms of scope, cost, schedule, and resource demand.

The most effective cost management system is one that ensures consultation with the stakeholders in all triple-constraint tradeoff decisions, and one that facilitates a full and prompt dissemination of the subsequent disposition of each change request to project personnel. Additionally, the determination of the variances between planned and actual values should not narrowly focus on the total project; instead, it should span all elements of the work breakdown schedule (WBS). As such, the current and/or variance of individual component resource expenditure and costs, as well as those for the total project, should always be at the disposal of the project stakeholders.

When the project is in its formative stages, very little information is available. Consequently, the accuracy and dependability of the estimate are very low. In other words, the risks of unforeseen and undesirable occurrences in the project are very high. Therefore, early plans and budgets are usually far from definitive and rarely predict the actual cost of individual components and the definitive cost of the total project. By contrast, at the early stages of the project, modifications to project plans can be formulated and conducted with minimal impact on cost and schedule. As the project proceeds into the various stages of growth, the cost of implementing modifications to the baseline plan increases substantially.

It would be unrealistic to expect good planning to eliminate the occurrence of all unexpected events. On the other hand, it is logical to expect a reduction in the magnitude and impact of project changes when the project is implemented with careful planning. Whereas a project with casually evolving plans contains many unexpected changes, a well-planned project has a significantly lower occurrence of unexpected events. It is therefore essential that the project manager conduct careful early planning to minimize the frequency and impact of project changes.

Even if the estimate of costs were reasonably accurate based on the detailed information available at the time of the early estimates, it is very likely that implementation costs will not match the planned costs due to changes in client requirements, design philosophy, and project environment. Thus, the data collected during the progress monitoring process are used to quantify the impact of the changes on the general direction of the project's overall performance.

The next step is to determine whether or not the performance variances and trends are significant. If variances are deemed significant, an adjustment of the triple constraints must be considered. This adjustment could be as simple as a change to the budget value. Alternately, in response to these new developments in the project environment, the adjustment could involve a change to the values of all triple constraints.

The basic administrative structure of a typical cost management system includes a change management board, a configuration management board, a change request form, and a change log. The change management board and configuration management board review the changes from a project management and a technological standpoint, respectively.

If the project is an external project, the change management board is composed of the project manger, the client liaison, technical personnel, and a contract officer. The change management board defines and implements the process of handling project change requests. During the implementation phase, the board ensures compliance with these established processes and procedures.

The change management board is composed of all the technical specialties represented in the project deliverable, the client representative, and the project management personnel. The configuration management board is charged with monitoring and documenting functional and physical characteristics of the deliverable's components as defined in the original project documents. Further, it is charged with managing the changes to these characteristics, optimizing the effects of the changes, and verifying conformance of the deliverable's attributes with the client's evolving specifications.

As an example, the change management board would review, in light of the client's current expectations, the impact that a change in a software module might have on the delivery date and on the total cost of the project. On the other hand, the configuration board would be concerned with the impact of these changes on the input/output structure of other modules, processing speed, maintenance complications, database duplication, and system complexity.

Procedural consistency in data collection and reporting will encourage the review of changes by the stakeholders, thus preventing ad-hoc implementation of changes. Figures 6-1 and 6-2 show a sample change request form

| FIGURE 6-1 | Change Request Form |

- Purpose
  - Standardize the Change Request Information
- Common Elements
  - Name of Requester
  - Requester's Organization
  - Date of Request
  - Description
  - Current Status
  - Action Requested
  - Change Request Number
  - Impact/Benefit of Change

FIGURE 6-2	Change Management Log

- Purpose
  - To Provide a Documented Record of the Change Requests Received during the Project
- Common Elements
  - Name of Requester
  - Requester's Organization
  - Date of Request
  - Description
  - Current Status
  - Action Requested
  - Change Request Number
  - Impact/Benefit of Change

and a typical format for the change management log. The change request form is the prescribed mechanism by which project changes are requested, approved, and announced. The change log is an historical account of the evolution history for scope, configuration, cost, and schedule. Maintaining the delicate balance between providing timely and complete flow of information to those who need it, while not overwhelming those who do not need to receive all the information, is essential in the cost management process. As each report is designed, defined, and distributed, special attention must be paid to the rationale for sending a particular report to a particular individual. The expected response from the recipient of that report should also be defined in detail. Finally, the cost management process need not be very elaborate, but needs to be formalized if the project is very small or if it involves only three or four people.

The necessary data and the essential tools of cost management activities include the current and updated WBS, cash flow constraints, details of current estimates and budgets, timely progress reports, accurate change reports, and cost management software responsive to the specific needs of that particular project. Project management should never allow the shortcomings and constraints of the project management software package to handicap the cost management process. Common solutions for overcoming shortcomings of the standard packages include opting for an add-on to the package or augmenting the software with another accounting software such as a spreadsheet or a database package. Of course, in the best interests of the project, selecting a different software package should always be an option.

If the final definitive budget is established from an early inaccurate estimate, the project stakeholders must be sensitive to the precision limitations of those estimates. In other words, the project estimate should be treated as a living document and updated as frequently as possible. Therefore, it is a reasonable to expect that the estimate of the project's total cost will vary with every estimate update, although a change in estimate will not necessarily trigger a change in budget.

The cost management process should not be treated as separate from the estimating and budgeting processes. Estimating and cost management should be treated as the integrated principal component of a process composed of the following revolving phases: developing the estimate, establishing the budget, managing the inevitable changes to the project, and making modifications to the estimate.

Experienced project managers are fully aware that treating the budget as an immovable object does not prevent cost variations; it simply discourages good record keeping, and makes data unavailable that might have isolated and explained the very possible future cost overruns. When the variance between the current and forecasted cost values exceeds the threshold set by the project manager, he or she should request that the budget be adjusted to the then-current value of the estimate. Understandably, some project environments preclude this process. In such organizations, project managers tend to add contingency buffers to the early estimates to mitigate the impact of future changes. On rare occasions, project managers do not explicitly show these buffers as such; they simply report the buffer-modified estimate as the definitive estimate. This practice is not recommended because it distorts the historical data collection necessary for improving future estimates.

During the implementation phase, the project manager will be placed in situations where he or she must make tradeoffs among the triple constraints of the project. The process of making tradeoffs is a consistent one if the project manager, together with the stakeholders, has determined the ranking of the triple constraints. Making such a ranking is very difficult for the stakeholders because they often hold all the triple constraints as important and somewhat unchangeable. However, the question to ask is, if it is imperative to make a choice between, for example, cost and schedule, which one will take priority over the other?

CAUSES OF CHANGE

The mission of a cost management system is not to control the costs at the original estimate level, which may or may not have been accurate.

Instead, the cost management process should be designed to manage the inevitable changes to the project with the least combined impact on the triple constraints of cost, schedule, and scope. Innumerable circumstances can change the project environment or its constraints. However, these circumstances can be grouped under five categories of sources of project changes:

- Changes in owner's needs
- Unexpected site conditions
- Evolution in the design philosophy
- Design or budget errors
- Implementation errors.

The first category of changes includes those generated by the client. The client may not have articulated the project objectives correctly or accurately at the inception of the project, and thus midway to completion of the project, the client sharpens or modifies the focus on the project's objectives. Such restatements of project objectives can sometimes be implemented without any appreciable effects on project plans, although usually they impact the baseline plan and cause delivery disruptions. Client revisions to the requirements can be technical in nature or they might restate the time or cost constraints. Time constraints, in turn, can set new delivery dates, limitations on cash flow, or restrictions on overall project expenditures.

Unexpected project conditions include items such as changes in operating system, hardware characteristics, site platforms, or site conditions, as well as occurrences such as strikes, tornados, or snowstorms. It goes without saying that unexpected events can never be prevented and their impact cannot be totally eliminated. However, the impact of unexpected events is minimized in projects that include a comprehensive risk management plan that is fully integrated with the planning process for cost, schedule, and scope.

The occurrence of major evolutions of design philosophy is fairly frequent in projects that depend on new technology. In projects that are highly dependent on cutting-edge innovations, the design team will often suggest a new design for the deliverables midstream into the project and in light of the current developments in that discipline. As much as these innovations are welcome in the deliverable, their introduction into the project plan will have a negative effect on the cost and schedule. Normally, the cost of remedial actions to deal with the changed circumstances can easily be attributed to the client and will become part of the new project budget.

A variation of the change in design philosophy is the category of cases where the project design team discovers a flaw in the basic design of the project. Depending on the character of this design flaw, corrective measures and product restructuring will impact the cost and schedule. The cost of recovery for this category of events is borne by the contractor if the contractor was responsible for the design and by the owner if the design was performed by the client or by a third-party designer. In most projects, there is an ongoing debate as to whether a design change was the result of an infusion of new technology or simply a bug-fixer.

Finally, in some cases the cost of the project and the delivery schedule have to be modified to account for errors in implementation such as substandard equipment, low quality components, or excessive error rate for a software component. If the project is an internal project, the client will absorb the cost increase for this last category of items as a matter of sponsorship. If the client participates in developing the project implementation activities, then the cost of recovery must be shared between the client and the contractor. In a cost-plus type of contract, determining the allocation of these additional costs is very delicate and complex, depending on the extent to which the client orchestrated the contractor's activities. However, if the project is an external fixed-price project, the cost of recovery from implementation errors is absorbed exclusively by the contractor.

When a change is observed in performance or in the external project's objective, the client and contractor will need to determine the category of the change, thereby determining who will absorb the resulting cost variances. This debate forms the basis for many client-contractor litigations.

FEED–FORWARD TECHNIQUE

There is no question that some of the data collected by the cost management system benefits future projects by establishing trends, baselines, and benchmarks. However, detailed cost reporting data also have substantial benefits for the current project. These benefits are primarily observed during the status meetings dealing with project change deliberations; detailed progress data facilitate more informed decision making. Additionally, in larger projects, data from earlier stages assist with the management of the latter stages. Having a formalized cost management process in place makes it possible to fine-tune the estimates of components developed during the latter stages based on the performance of earlier components. Figure 6-3 shows the reported progress for one element of the WBS. Figure 6-4 shows the forecast values for a similar component that will be implemented during the second half of the project.

| FIGURE 6-3 | Simple Schedule Network Forecasting |

Assumptions:

- **Expenditures Vary Linearly with Progress**
- **Expenditures Are Uniform throughout the Activity**
- **Learning and Experience Curves Do Not Apply**
- **Activities Are Not Calendar Dependent**
- **Activities A1 and A2 Are Nearly Identical**
- **Activity A1 Was Just Finished**
- **Activity A2 Is Scheduled**

| FIGURE 6-4 | Simple Forecasting |

- **Activity A1 Was Just Completed**
  - With 82% of the Estimated Resources
  - At 109% of the Estimated Time
- **The Estimate for Activity A2 Must Be Modified to Reflect**
  - 18% Decrease in Resources
  - 9% Increase in Time
  - ?% Change in Total A2 Cost

The benefits of the availability of detailed project data extend even further. Using a sophisticated cost monitoring and management system and the feed-forward technique, a seasoned project manager is able to adjust the estimated progress rate of the second half of a component based on the performance of the first half of that same component. Literature shows that in most projects the trends established during the first 15 percent of the project's life[1] are expected to continue through the life of the project unless major redirection is applied. Of course, if the project has not implemented a sophisticated progress monitoring system, these trends will go largely undetected.

IMPACT OF SCHEDULE ON COST

During the early planning stages, the estimate is predicated on certain assumptions about the pace of the project and the scope and quality of the characteristics of the deliverables. Accordingly, because cost is directly impacted by changes in duration and scope, managing cost will always have to be done in concert with managing scope and schedule. Even if the baseline project scope remains unchanged, changes to the project schedule will bring corresponding changes in the resource expenditure and cost of the project.

A typical construction, industrial, or process project has the following generic phases:
- Preliminary design
- Detailed design
- Prototype development
- Construction
- Acceptance testing
- Turnover.

A typical software system development project is generally composed of the following phases:
- Requirement statement
- Requirement analysis
- System design
- Implementation
- Unit testing
- Integration
- System testing
- Delivery.

The traditional and simplest form of conducting projects is sequentially and by phases—one after another. This form of project execution minimizes the errors introduced into the project deliverable due to rapid implementation, hasty communication, and workplace congestion. Figure 6-5 shows

FIGURE 6-5	Project Stages

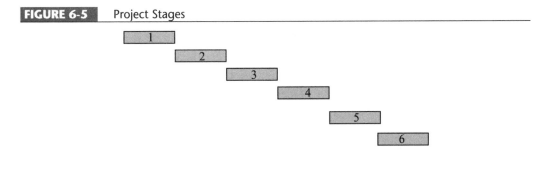

Traditional Sequencing of Activities

traditional project sequencing, which produces the lowest cost of all options, although it takes the longest of all sequencing options to complete the project.

Since projects are intended to develop deliverables that must ultimately satisfy a specific business need, there is always pressure on the project manager to finish the project sooner. Therefore, it is important to be aware of the implications of compressing the duration of a project. Experience in construction and industrial projects has shown that there is a threshold beyond which project duration cannot be compressed. This threshold is normally about 50 percent of the optimum duration and is commonly referred to as the *crash point*. The goal in compressing projects is to compress the project duration to a point just above the crash point.

There are two ways of achieving a shorter duration for the project: (1) by modifying the project scheduling network through sequencing of various activities and phases, or (2) by shortening the individual critical path activities. The network modification is performed after a careful review of the network logic and segmenting bigger activities into smaller ones so that a tighter network can be achieved. If the project duration is compressed by fine-tuning the sequence of the phases, the nature and composition of these components must be changed to accommodate an overlapping execution sequence for the components. Thus, shorter duration for the project is achieved by breaking the project into as many phases as possible, with each phase starting as soon as possible, but not necessarily after completion of the full complement of the logical predecessor phase. This technique is called fast tracking in construction projects, concurrent engineering in industrial and process projects, and rapid application development in software system development projects (see Figure 6-6).

An example of this technique in the construction industry is releasing the design documents in small increments so that construction of the facility can start well before the entire facility is fully designed, rather than waiting until all components are designed. The builder will pour the concrete for the foundation while the design for the steel building frame is ongoing. An example of this technique in the software industry is beginning to develop individual components as soon as a discrete portion of the requirements is defined. Another example in the software industry is testing individual modules as they are developed, rather than waiting to test all components together when the software development is fully complete. It bears highlighting that individual testing of the modules may not be as cost-effective as testing all the modules at the same time.

FIGURE 6-6 Project Stages

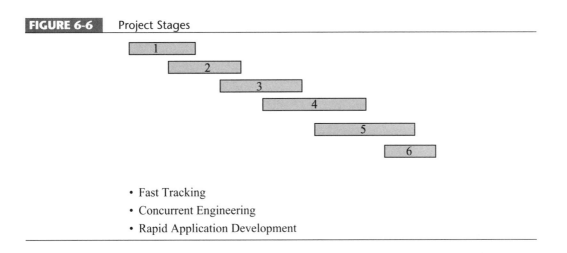

- Fast Tracking
- Concurrent Engineering
- Rapid Application Development

There is an inherent drawback in overlapping phases that are logically serial phases. When such phases overlap, the resource intensity impact, the cost impact, and even the schedule impact of recovery from errors and reworks are drastic. Notwithstanding, the incentive to use the method of overlapping phases is that if the project is implemented smoothly, the delivery date is far more attractive. Of course, this expectation does not always materialize.

The second means of reducing the project duration involves compressing the critical path. This is achieved by compressing selected activities of the critical path—not by reducing the number of activities in the chain. Compressing individual critical path activities would involve adding more shifts or a larger crew size to a given activity to reduce the duration of that activity, and therefore, the project. Experience in construction, process, and industrial projects has shown that there is a minimum cost for each task; this minimum cost will occur when the optimum crew size and shift duration are observed during implementation of that task. Consequently, it is hoped that the original project cost baseline was derived from the original elemental cost baseline which, in turn, was developed using optimum crew size for those tasks. By extension, the baseline duration is hopefully the optimum duration. Then, if performance duration other than the optimum duration is chosen for the project, the effects of such duration compression on cost can be determined methodically and consistently using a formulation similar to the normalized curve depicted in Figure 6-7.

As the estimate for each element and module of the project is refined, the optimum duration and minimum cost of that element must continually

FIGURE 6-7   Cost–Duration Relationship

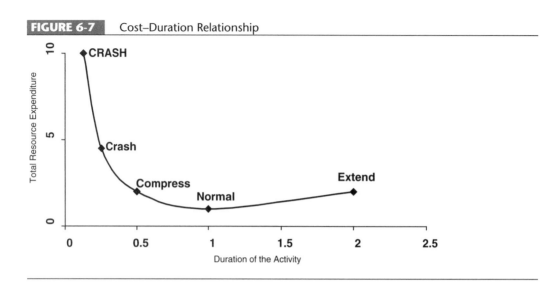

be reviewed, or at least used as a base of reference. Figure 6-7 shows a generic depiction of the relationship between the effort required for the task—the cost—and the duration of implementation of that task. As a rule of thumb, if the duration of the element is halved, the total effort for the activity will double. In other words, there is always a cost penalty for reducing the elemental duration from what is considered to be the optimum. (Reducing the duration of the element by 50 percent from its optimum is drastic. Normally, clients ask for a 10 percent or 20 percent reduction in duration.)

Ironically, sometimes it comes as a surprise to project managers that when the activity's crew size is increased in order to increase the pace of progress, the increased pace is accompanied by a reduction in efficiency. This reduction in efficiency is the result of hasty implementation, physical congestion, and increases in communications errors. Once the number of team members is increased to speed up the project, the lines of communications are increased dramatically, in addition to the likelihood of miscommunications, duplication of work, and implementation errors.

Notwithstanding these considerations, if the client wants the project duration to be compressed, that is how the project manager must proceed—even though project compression carries a cost penalty. In construction projects, increasing the number of workers causes physical congestion, causing slowdowns and potential safety hazards. In software projects, the detrimental effects of a larger crew are subtler and less visible, but present nonetheless.

To illustrate the concept of optimum duration, consider an activity where it takes five programmers six days to develop the code for a particular database. If the duration were forced to four days, nine programmers might be required to finish this project. To extend this illustration to the extreme, if the duration were forced to three days, twenty programmers would be required for the same task (see Figure 6-8).

At the other end of the spectrum, if there are resource shortages or cash flow constraints, then the project must be implemented using a smaller and less-than-optimum crew, thereby increasing the time it takes to complete the project. This deviation from optimum will also increase the total effort of the project, although the effect would not be as pronounced as the effect of compression. If the duration is doubled, the total cost and effort will also double. The reduction in efficiency caused by an increase in duration is the result of penalties involved in more-than-normal start-stop sequences of the processes, reduced team interaction, and deterioration in organizational and individual memory with respect to work details and learning curves.

The literature contains extensive historical data regarding the cost penalty for compressing or expanding the schedule network for construction, industrial, and process projects. Therefore, the cost variances for changing project schedules can be computed fairly accurately and based on industry-specific data, and not necessarily based on the ratios shown in Figures 6-7 and 6-8. If the project is in the software and system development area, given the absence of satisfactory historical data, the generic ratios stated in these illustrations can be used as a good first approximation for this relationship. If detailed historical data are available, discipline-specific mathematical or graphic relationships can be developed for the optimum duration of the projects and thus depict the lowest cost for a specific project conducted in a specific environment.

Some project managers, particularly in software and system development projects, anticipate and react to the possibility of network compression

| FIGURE 6-8 | Example of Activity Compression |

Programmers	*Duration*	*Effort*
5	6 Days	30 Worker Days
7	5 Days	35 Worker Days
11	4 Days	44 Worker Days
20	3 Days	60 Worker Days

requests by embedding buffers in the original schedule logic. These embedded buffers are created during the planning stages by the inclusion of many sequential activities performed with an understaffed team and using very few parallel activities. Then, once the client makes the expected request for duration compression, the project manager announces that some serial activities can be done in parallel with the proper personnel to accommodate the client's wishes at minimal additional cost.

This tactic, although proactive and sometimes effective, can be highly explosive. If and when the client becomes aware that the original schedule—and the subsequent compression—were arbitrary, the project manager loses all credibility and the ability to effectively explain future project variances to the client. The best policy is to develop the original cost and schedule based on optimum crew size, cost, and duration. Then, as project circumstances such as resource skill, resource availability, and client business needs present themselves, the budget and schedule can be changed accordingly.

LIFECYCLE COSTS

There is some overlap between lifecycle cost analysis and value analysis. For the purposes of this chapter, they will be treated together. The purpose of value analysis is to develop a product design strategy that will result in the lowest cost for that particular function or product. The value-analysis process depends on a detailed understanding of the client's needs and desires in terms of the functionality of the deliverable. Then, on the basis of the detailed definition of the product's desired functions, the value analysis process produces the specifications for the appropriate hardware or software. A value-analysis process might recommend traditional components for the function or develop a new design to reduce the cost while being responsive to the client's needs.

The project management lifecycle cost analysis process incorporates the cost not only of delivering the project, but also of enhancing, maintaining, and ultimately decommissioning it. Decommissioning or disposal costs must be part of owner's considerations in cost evaluations during the planning and project selection phases. However, these issues are not always part of the design considerations for the contractor/vendor organizations, unless they are explicitly listed as objectives of the project at-hand.

The advantage of using a lifecycle cost analysis is that it puts the overall cost of a product into focus. Sometimes, a product that has the lowest delivery cost may not be the best choice if the overall lifecycle cost of that deliverable is higher than that of other products designed to meet the same set of objectives.

An example of a balance between the implementation costs and lifecycle costs is installing a pump that is smaller and less expensive than the one originally envisioned. The motivation for this change might be that the smaller pump is faster to install. However, this change must be made with the full recognition that the operating and repair cost of this pump will be much higher than the one originally designed. Therefore, for comparison purposes, it is necessary to compare not just the installation costs, but rather the sum of the purchase cost and the lifetime operating costs for these two pumps.

Finally, early delivery of the project is not without making sacrifices in cost, quality, and scope. A balance needs to be struck between the overall impact of the financial benefits of early delivery and the long-term penalties of a slightly impure deliverable. An example of such balance in a software project is that the software may lack some of the desired features and even include some unresolved software errors if it is delivered to the client sooner. This expediency will probably accompany the additional costs for more detailed training for operational personnel and debugging and maintaining the system. Likewise, the cost comparison should be made between the sum of the development cost and the lifetime costs for debugging, training, and maintenance for the two options under review.

Many organizations insist on a value analysis and a lifecycle cost analysis as part of the original cost-estimating phase. In the same fashion that the estimate and the planning data should be treated as living documents, the value analysis and the lifecycle analysis should be refreshed frequently during the life of the project. At the very least, lifecycle analyses should be refreshed when the triple constraints go through significant changes or when more details about lifecycle issues become available.

IMPACT OF PROJECT RISK

For every project, there are possible occurrences that impact the scope, quality, cost, and schedule. As part of the initial planning, a risk assessment must be conducted to determine the possible impact of these occurrences. Once the impact of these occurrences is determined, the project manager is able to decide how to deal with such probabilities. The project manager may choose to accept the risk or put provisions in place for dealing with the occurrence of such risks. These provisions may include assigning project personnel to monitor and handle this issue on a contingency basis or simply developing contingency funds that will be available for use if and when the risk event materializes. The important issue is that the project must have a proactive and comprehensive risk management plan in place to mitigate the impact of unexpected events.

The basic form of risk management is to consider only those risk events that are totally out of the control of the project team, such as strikes, floods, and tornados. A modified view of risk management includes risks of undesirable occurrences from all sources. This expanded view of risk includes consideration of impacts of and remedies for cost overrun, schedule delay, physical defects, and performance shortcomings of the deliverable. In developing a risk management plan, the project manager must identify risks that are consistent with corporate policy and with good project management practices. More importantly, the same risk identification structure must be used consistently in all projects.

One method of recognizing the financial impact of and planning for risk events is to determine a statistical monetary value for the risk and then somehow incorporate those risk-related expenses into the project estimate. Implementation of this simple solution begins with determining the probability of occurrence and the cost impact of occurrence for each risk event. The product of these two values is the funds representing the statistical impact of that particular risk. Once this calculation is conducted for all risk events, the total funds representing the statistical cost impact can either be incorporated into the project budget or placed in a separate fund specifically earmarked for dealing with the results of risk events (see Figure 6-9). Alternately, depending on the funding structure of the project, risk-related funds

FIGURE 6-9 Risk Contingency Funds: A Simple Example

Risk Event	Probability	Impact	Statistical Impact
Risk 1	10%	$100,000	$10,000
Risk 2	5%	$20,000	$1,000
Risk 3	12%	$80,000	$9,600
Risk 4	15%	$200,000	$30,000
Risk 5	5%	$150,000	$7,500
......			
......			
......			

Total Risk Related Contingency Funds $180,000

might become either part of a client reserve or part of project contingency funds.

Although it is every project manager's dream that the project will follow the plans smoothly and precisely, the challenges that the project manager will likely face involve handling issues brought on by unexpected events. These events usually accompany a negative impact to the triple constraints of cost, schedule, and scope. The mission of the project manager then becomes searching for the best compromise in the values of the triple constraints. This objective should not be to hold the cost to what was planned many weeks, months, or even years ago, but rather to provide acceptable values for schedule and scope while minimizing the increase in the cost of the project. This process should always be characterized as managing the cost, and not necessarily controlling it.

NOTE

1. Anonymous, *Parametric Estimating Handbook*, 2nd ed. (Washington, DC: US Department of Defense, 1999).

CHAPTER 7

External Projects

For strategic reasons, organizations sometimes choose to acquire resources from outside the organization for a project. This process is aptly called *outsourcing* or *contracting*. The decision to outsource depends primarily on the organization's strategic objectives and factors such as the prospective internal team's competencies and the infrastructure characteristics of the division sponsoring the project. Other contributing factors include market conditions and the organization's competitive aspirations. Some organizations opt for external projects in the hope of getting immediate access to specialized skills and/or equipment and gaining expertise in that specific area through exposure and observation. The external project concept is often used as a subtle mechanism for transforming the culture of the organization. Finally, some argue that external projects are less costly to the organization.

The disadvantage of outsourcing is that the organization is denied the opportunity to improve and enhance the operational capability and competency of its internal workforce. Further, the company might lose direct involvement and control of the project's execution. More importantly, an external project may jeopardize the trade secrets and the proprietary details of the organization's best practices. Finally, the cost of executing external projects is sometimes higher when both the tangible and intangible costs are considered.

An undesirable side effect of outsourcing is the self-perpetuating effect on the organization, primarily because frequently there is very little, if any, institutional memory from the execution of the project, in spite of wishful expectations to the contrary. Therefore, because the project was conducted with a team outside the organizational structure, the stage is set to have future projects outsourced also.

External projects sometimes put pressure on the client to be more specific in defining the physical attributes and performance expectations of the final deliverable. Ironically, it is often the lack of desired competency in a technical area of the project that is the primary impetus for resorting to external projects. Therefore, having the client provide a detailed articulation of objectives and specifications becomes an impossible task. Because of these constraints, contractors often develop, as the first phase of project implementation, the project specifications by interpreting the client's objectives.

SPECIFICATIONS

Project planning and its ultimate implementation are normally conducted based on the detailed definition of the project's scope and objectives. Such detailed and formal specifications are frequently drafted only for external projects. However, for purposes of cost management and organizational memory, it is desirable to develop and maintain specifications for internal as well as external projects. Project specifications are included in the contract for external projects and in the authorization memo for internal projects.

Ideally, project specifications highlight what will be delivered to the client once the project is completed. It is less useful if the project specifications outline the project's activities without any major emphasis on the deliverables. The specifications documents are the most formalized articulation of the client's wishes and desires. The specifications document includes all the necessary technical data to plan and implement the project. It provides details of all items that are needed or desired, as well as details of all items that are considered undesirable or unacceptable. Further, the specifications outline items that are necessary for the project's success but will be fabricated, developed, or delivered by the efforts of another project. Finally, the specifications may include details of materials, equipment, services, procedures, and tools.

The detailed information for project specifications is presented in written, tabular, and graphic formats. To some extent, the choice of the format is dictated by the nature of information. For example, a graphic format is most efficient in conveying the arrangement, size, and location of physical components, while spreadsheets and tables would be the vehicle of choice for portraying numerical relationships. Naturally, text would be most appropriate for verbal descriptions of objectives, activities, performance criteria, and strategic issues.

It is very difficult, if not virtually impossible, to produce complete and flawless specifications, as evidenced by the revisions issued to contract documents as early as the bidding process. Therefore, one should anticipate changes to the specifications, to some extent, during the life of the project. These changes include clarifications and modifications to the project's scope, quality, expected cost, and desired duration. As the project evolves into more mature stages, these changes should be reflected in the WBS, the specifications, and other planning facets of the project. To facilitate comprehension of and compliance with the specifications, all facets of the project deliverables must be quantified to the extent practicable. Accordingly, attempts should be made to quantify deliverable qualifiers such as friendly, robust, smooth, and aesthetically pleasing.

There are three types of specifications: design, performance, and functional. *Design* or *product specifications* provide details of what is to be delivered in terms of physical characteristics or detailed tasks intended to contribute to a product or a service. An example of this type of specifications is the client providing details of how web pages should be designed, what graphics should be used in the various web pages, and how many records the database should contain. As such, the risk of performance and applicability rests directly with the client. Design specifications in contracting and purchasing:

- Provide details of what is to be done in terms of physical characteristics
- Place the risk of performance and applicability on the client.

Performance specifications are drafted with performance or generic characteristics in mind, and define measurable capabilities that the deliverable must achieve in terms of operational capabilities. An example of this type of specifications is the client spelling out the access speed, error rate, and general linkage characteristics of the web site. The project team then drafts plans that have the proper technical features so that the deliverable satisfies the client's performance expectations. Naturally, the risk of performance is borne by the project team while the risk of applicability is borne by the client. Performance specifications in contracting and purchasing:

- Specify measurable capabilities that the end product must achieve in terms of operational characteristics
- Place the risk of performance on the contractor
- Place the risk of applicability on the client.

A set of *functional specifications* is probably the most logical mode of responding to the "wants and needs" of the client. However, it burdens the client with the task of defining in very clear terms the basic objective of the final product. At the same time, this mode of specification development will empower the creativity of the project team in using innovative techniques to meet or exceed the client's expectations. Functional specifications in contracting and purchasing:

- Describe the end use of the item

- Stimulate competition among vendors
- Place the risk of performance and applicability on the contractor.

An example of this type of specifications is the client providing the contractor with the general business plan and the expected business outcome. The contractor then develops a set of detailed plans and specifications so that the project meets those business needs. Under this mode of operation, it is entirely possible that the contractor will communicate the specifications to the client, but that is usually just to keep the client informed, and not necessarily for approval purposes.

In some cases, the client and the project team collectively develop project specifications. Even though this is a useful policy, it involves the risk of blending project specifications with project implementation details and project scheduling techniques. In some software and system development projects, the implementation team develops the project specifications by interpreting and analyzing the client's needs and objectives. This practice also blurs the line between the client's goals and the project team's objectives. With an overlap between client-generated and contractor-generated material, it is very difficult to analyze and evaluate the causes of cost and duration overruns.

Finally, cost and duration overruns are usually accompanied by a gradual change in project scope, therefore complicating the identification of a logical baseline for the project. If the scope changes are not documented, or if they are not managed in a formalized and consistent fashion, one more level of difficulty will be added to the task of managing the resulting cost impact of the project changes. This continuous shifting of the baseline is sometimes referred to as *scope creep*. Scope creep is endemic in projects that are conducted as cost-plus, in organizations with few original project objectives, or in projects with plans and specifications formulated on the basis of "fuzzy" objectives. However, a certain amount of scope modification should be expected in most projects, either external or internal.

CONTRACTS

A *contract* is the legal instrument by which an organization acquires products and services from an outside source. To define the responsibilities and rewards of both parties, a contract must conform to its legal definition:

- An understanding enforceable by law
- Formed between two or more parties
- Formed for money or exchange as an end result

- Legal in substance
- Requires an offer and an acceptance.

It is in the light of these considerations that a contract is drafted, signed, and enforced. Notwithstanding, for the purposes of a project, a contract is considered an administrative mechanism by which the project is conducted by personnel who reside outside the corporate boundaries of the client's organization.

A casual definition of a contract is:

A binding agreement to acquire goods and services toward the goals of a project.

Contract documents for a project are composed of two major parts, administrative and technical (see Figure 7-1). The administrative part deals with the legal responsibilities of both parties and the processes and procedures for enforcing the various contract clauses. The second part deals with the technical content of the project. The technical content, and the issues that directly affect the implementation pace, are the focus of this chapter.

There are two basic forms of project contracts:

1. Lump-sum (fixed-price)
2. Cost-plus fixed fee (time and material).

A *fixed-price* or *lump-sum* contract requires detailed specifications. Usually, the contractor with the lowest price is chosen for that particular project. The contractor's offer is called a *bid* and the contractor chosen for the job is referred to as the *winner of the contract*. In this mode of contracting, the prospective contractor offers to deliver the project deliverables for a fixed price. The contractor guarantees the fixed price and thus assumes all financial risk in implementing that project. That is, of course, if the initial set of client objectives and project specifications are spelled out in sufficient detail and the

FIGURE 7-1	Contract Documents

- Envisions All Physical and *Administrative* Possibilities.

  Sets Guidelines:
  – General Conditions
  – Special Conditions
- Presents the *Technical* Data for This Job
  – Text
  – Tabular
  – Graphic

project environment remains reasonably stable during the life of the project. Under ideal circumstances, this type of contract gives the contractor full incentives to avoid waste, reduce costs, and increase profits.

The following are characteristics of a lump-sum contract:
- Requires accurate and detailed design
- Minimizes initial uncertainties in cost and quality
- Is safe for the owner if the scope stays unchanged
- Has low profits for the contractor if the scope stays unchanged
- Is potentially explosive for both if the scope is changed.

Again, the lump-sum contract is most appropriate for projects whose scope and specifications are outlined precisely and where there is only a small chance of changes in scope and specifications. If there are midstream changes to the scope and specifications, the contract has to be modified to reflect a new price. The new price and other conditions of the contract are negotiated between the contractor and the client at the onset of these changes in the project environment. It is during, and as a result of, these contract modifications that the advisability of the lump-sum contract comes under scrutiny.

The second type of contracts is called *cost-plus,* or *time-and-material.* In this form of contracting, the contractor is selected on the basis of technical capability and on the the lowest price per unit of labor, equipment, overhead, and materials. The owner then directs the contractor to perform the various tasks of the project. The contractor is paid the amount of time for labor and equipment as well as the volume of materials spent on this project in accordance with client's instructions (see Figure 7-2).

In construction and industrial projects, *unit-price* is a third basic form of contracting. This form is a mixture of the two basic forms described above.

FIGURE 7-2   Types of Contracts—Expanded

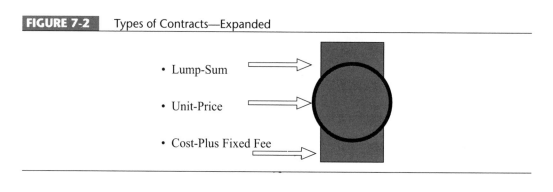

In effect, unit price represents a fixed price for a small element of the project. Under this type of contract, the contractor submits a bid for each of the many small elements of the project. The contractor then gets paid for the number of these units that are used for the project. Examples of unit-pricing elements are: one specific test using one specific testing machine, one line of code, one web page, one yard of concrete, one module of training, etc.

Cost-plus contracts have the following characteristics:

- Contractor's profit is always protected
- The owner has the freedom to modify the scope frequently
- The project estimate becomes a vague target
- There is little incentive for the contractor to be productive or expedient.

Experience has shown that these basic forms of contracts do not address challenges that present themselves during the life of the project. Consequently, organizations award contracts that use one of the basic forms with modifiers that reward and/or restrict the behavior of the contractor.

Examples of modifiers for cost-plus or unit-cost contracts are:

- Guaranteed maximum
- Overrun cost sharing
- Underrun profit sharing
- Bonus for underrun
- Penalty for overrun
- Bonus for early delivery
- Penalty for late delivery
- Reduced fee for being late or over budget
- No fee after estimated date and cost.

These modifiers are intended to give the client the flexibility to modify the project specifications midstream, causing the least possible impact on project performance in cost and duration. These modifiers are also intended to provide incentives to the contractor to be efficient, responsive, and exceptionally mindful of the best interests of the client—of course, not to the exclusion of the contractor's objectives of receiving the highest possible return on investment.

The contract management procedures outline the process of monitoring the contractor's performance within the boundaries established by the contract and in light of the project's technical objectives. While contract management planning documents include procedures and policies to ensure compliance with the contract, they also afford a reasonable amount of flexibility for minor changes in the deliverables.

RESPONSE TO SPECIFICATIONS

The role of specifications is minimal in cost-plus contracts. There is no need to develop them fully during the contract award phase because the contractor will be paid based on how much time and effort are spent, rather than what is produced. Therefore, a cost-plus contractor is chosen on the basis of perceived capability and potential reliability, and not necessarily a promised total cost or delivery date. Given the nature of cost-plus contracts, sometimes the first assignment of the contractor is to develop the specifications and estimates for the project; it is almost certain that the same contractor will implement the resulting specifications.

On the other hand, the role of specifications is pivotal in fixed-price contracts, because the specifications will form the basis for the estimate, the bid, and the eventual award. Midstream modification of a fixed-price contract is difficult, time-consuming, and potentially expensive. Therefore, fixed-price contracts should be awarded only if the specifications are exceptionally accurate and the likelihood of changes in the specifications is extraordinarily low.

When reviewing specifications, the project manager must make an effort to understand all the client's objectives and the underlying reasons for a particular facet of the deliverable. Ideally, this philosophy should be the guiding light for all types of projects on the premise that it fosters client-contractor partnership and trust. Although the implementation of such a congenial and trusting environment is possible, it must be approached with sensitivity to the fact that the obligations and the reward system for the contractor personnel and client personnel, as delineated in the contract, are different and possibly in conflict. Therefore, this philosophy is not practiced fully and widely in contracting environments because it subtly impacts the contracting strategy, bidding outcomes, and award circumstances.

Partly prompted by competitive contracting strategy and partly in an effort to be seen as accommodating, prospective fixed-price contractors often offer to comply with all the conditions set forth in contract specifications. The reinforcing element for this behavior is that the clients often regard such conformist behavior in a positive light. Notwithstanding, changes to the project scope during the life of the project would be grounds for renegotiating the contract. It is not known how many contractors could have predicted the nature and extent of the contract's scope changes and chose not to confront the client regarding the quality of the specifications. However, it is commonly accepted that contractors of fixed-price contracts tend to prosper when there are a lot of change orders during the life of the contract.

Ideally, if there are flaws or omissions in the statements of scope, specifications, or desired procedures presented to a potential contractor or the project manager, the contractor or project manager should respond by:

- Asking questions
- Listing assumptions
- Taking exceptions
- Making suggestions.

The responses to specifications review (expanded in Figure 7-3) serve the best interests of the client and the best long-term interests of the contractor, although sometimes there is a conflict between the short-term and long-term interests of the contractor. The recommended responses are to ask questions when there is ambiguity, to list assumptions when the specifications are incomplete, to take exceptions when an objective is unattainable, and to make suggestions when the specifications need improvements. Traditionally, contractors' responses are more in line with compliance rather than the seemingly confrontational responses outlined in Figure 7-3. In some cases, the clients reinforce the contractor's passive behavior by rewarding those who exhibit lack of feedback and punishing those who provide feedback that is not entirely complimentary (see Figure 7-4).

FIGURE 7-3   Response to Communications

- Ask Questions
  - Smart Questions
  - Dumb Questions
- Take Exception
  - Let the Client Know That
    - The Approach Is Impossible
    - The Deliverable Is Unattainable
- Make Suggestions
  - Highlight Your Expertise by Offering Alternatives
- List Assumptions
  - Develop Lists for
    - Inclusions
    - Exclusions
    - Deliverables of Other Groups Needed for This Project

| FIGURE 7-4 | Consequences: Responding to Communications |

- The Entrepreneurial Approach Would Be to Provide Feedback in All Four Categories
- The Safe Approach Would Be to Give Minimal Feedback.

- *If Your Response Uncovers a Flaw in the Original Communication, or Sheds Light on Alternatives, You Might Be Rewarded by the Client*
- *If Your Response Indicates Lack of Planning and/or Lack of Knowledge, You Might Be Punished by the Client.*

In rare cases, the client forms partnerships with the contractor for the purposes of the project. In such cases, the potential contractor is encouraged to behave as part of the client's team and he or she is rewarded for behaving in the project's best interest—although it may sometimes appear to be at odds with his or her short-term interests. It is in these latter cases that the client tends to reap the benefits of the contractor's experience and dedication, while the contractor is allowed to earn a reasonable return on investment.

BIDDING

A bid and an estimate are two entirely different things, although sometimes clients and contractors use these two terms interchangeably. An *estimate* is a detailed account of what it will cost to deliver a product based on specific information of the actual cost of materials and equipment, the actual salary of personnel, and a realistic characterization of the overhead structure of the contractor's organization. Depending on the circumstances, an estimate may or may not include overhead costs, indirect costs, and profit.

By comparison, the *bid* or *contract price* may not necessarily include details of the various components of the cost estimate that have formed the basis for the bid. Even if the bid includes details of components such as direct costs, indirect costs, overhead, contingency, and return on investment, these figures are not necessarily actual or realistic. The amounts included in a bid simply represent the amounts that the contractor is planning to charge for labor, materials, and equipment, indirect costs, overhead costs, contingencies, and the all-important return on investment. These values are usually modified for the purposes of the bid.

It bears repeating that an estimate and a bid are fundamentally different; the transition from an estimate to a bid is a business decision based on the probability of occurrence of unexpected events, desirable or undesirable, as well as on the bidder's motivation.

Generally, the profit margin in a contract must be in concert with the number of bidders for the same job, primarily because prospective contractors, in an effort to be the lowest bidder, reduce the overall profit to its lowest possible margin. As Figure 7-5 shows, when there are many bidders for the same job, the expected profit margin is very low, while for jobs with very few bidders, the profit margin increases accordingly.[1,2] Obviously, the most desirable situation for a contractor is one where there are very few bidders for the contract.

A low profit margin increases the bidder's chances of success, although bidding a job below realistic cost does not necessarily guarantee wining the contract. On the other hand, an extraordinarily high profit margin reduces the chances of the bidder's success, although bidding a job with high profit margin does not necessarily eliminate all chances of winning the contract.

The presence of a contract creates an environment of delineated objectives that sometimes precludes a common focus on the project by the client and the contractor. Various efforts in the areas of partnering have provided a less adversarial contract environment, but don't forget that contractors and clients have two different sets of motivations and objectives. In a contracting situation, the bidder's objectives are to win the contract, complete the project

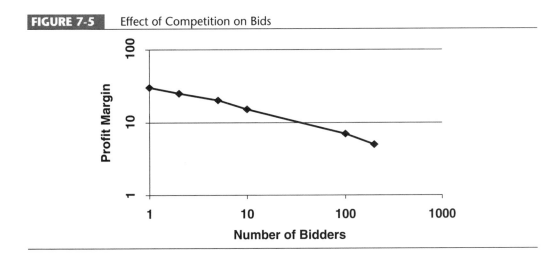

FIGURE 7-5   Effect of Competition on Bids

quickly, receive prompt payment, and realize a good profit. On the other hand, the owner's objectives are to pay the lowest price possible for the earliest delivery date and for a responsive performance. The number of lawsuits that clients and contractors file against one another demonstrates this adversarial attitude, which stems from the disparity between the client's business objectives and the contractor's operating objectives.

PROJECT COSTS

Normally when an internal project is commissioned, the cost of the project does not include anything beyond the cost of assigning personnel and equipment to the project. The distinction between direct cost and indirect cost tends to be more important in organizations that conduct external projects. However, the real cost of the project includes other cost components such as indirect costs, overhead, and return on investment. Therefore, a sensitivity to the issues of indirect and overhead costs allows an internal project manager to assess the real costs of an internal project and to compare two internal projects on the basis of direct costs. When comparing an external project with an internal project, care should be taken to include the necessary additional cost items so that a more rational and logical comparison can be made between an internal project and an external one.

Direct Costs

Direct costs are those costs that are directly attributable to the project, such as salaries, travel, and buying or renting equipment for the explicit use of the project. It is important to remember that if personnel or equipment are shared between projects, only a portion of the salary and purchase cost should be included, to the extent that the resources are used for the activities of a particular project. One popular way of testing the direct cost elements is to consider the cost of those people and equipment that actually came in contact with the project deliverable, and for the duration that they came in contact with the deliverable.

Indirect Costs

Indirect costs include the costs of infrastructure for human and physical resources that are necessary for the project's smooth operation, again to the extent that the resources are indirectly associated with the project. Indirect costs include sick leave, vacation, training, and retirement benefits for the employees. Indirect costs also include portions of the salary of supervisory personnel. Other indirect items are portions of the cost of administrative support, phone system, faxes, computers, rent, insurance, taxes, and utilities.

Direct costs and indirect costs are items that can easily be related to the cost of implementing components of the deliverables. Thus, they are an integral part of the cost estimate of an external project and, therefore, should not be subject to negotiations or alterations during the contract award phases.

Overhead

Overhead items are somewhat removed from the project, although they are necessary for the successful conduct of the project. They include compensation of the organization's senior management and the cost of infrastructure necessary for supporting their activities. Overhead items also include the cost of preparing unsuccessful proposals, general marketing and public relations, and ongoing innovative ventures of the organization. The extent to which these overhead costs are charged to a project is always the subject of extensive debate. Moreover, a project is very unattractive if it does not produce a profit, or its euphemistic equivalent, return on investment. The extent of return on investment is also another issue of contract negotiation.

This loosely knit bundle of cost categories is always under scrutiny by the prospective client, and an issue of negotiation at the time of the award for a contract for an external project.

Allowance

An *allowance* is a lump-sum estimate that is assigned to certain project items. Usually the basis for using an allowance, instead of a detailed estimate, is that although the project manager predicts that a certain cost will be incurred, the project manager has also made the determination that the elements cannot be identified with any accuracy, or a detailed estimate is not necessary.

An example of the use of an allowance is the estimate for travel expenses. If the project manager knows that it is likely that the team will have to travel to the installation sites about a dozen times, then rather than estimating the cost of airline tickets and hotel costs for each separate trip, the project manager includes an allowance of $75,000 for travel expenses. Other examples are the costs of office supplies, phone calls, and software licenses. The allowance method is somewhat akin to an analogous estimate for that particular component of the project. An allowance should be used infrequently and even then only for those cost elements that represent a very small percentage of the overall cost of the project.

Contingency

The terms *contingency* and *client-reserve* are often used interchangeably to refer to two different kinds of buffer funds. For the purposes of this book, the term *contingency* is used for the funds that are added to the estimate to compensate for those estimate inaccuracies caused by uncertainties in project details. The term *client-reserve* refers to those funds that are set aside to subsidize the cost changes brought on by changes in client objectives. In some ways, contingency funds and reserve funds are akin to allowances, except that contingency funds deal with unknown issues. Sometimes, clients establish contingency and reserve funds even for internal projects to keep some formality in budget development and the eventual cost management.

The definition and purpose of contingency funds will become a blurred concept if there are regular or occasional changes to the project scope during the life of the contract. The definition becomes even more blurred if the risk-related contingency funds are rolled together with other contingency funds in the same account. Contingency funds are not intended for covering the cost of errors in design, implementation, omission, and miscalculation in estimating. These items should be addressed as part of a renegotiation for a new budget or a new contract, or amendments thereof. Client-reserve refers to those funds that the client sets aside as part of the organizational budget, but apart from the contract budget, to accommodate project cost changes caused by changes in project environment or objectives.

Traditionally, the magnitude of contingency funds is 10 percent to 50 percent, depending on the volume of information available at the time of the estimate. This range is deemed appropriate because it is generally anticipated that when a project is advertised for bid, the objectives and statements of specification possess a reasonable accuracy of about 20 percent. The magnitude of client reserve funds varies from 10 percent to 50 percent, depending on the level of innovation required in the project, which in turn might trigger major design changes.[3–6] The level of client reserves also depends on the extent to which the client team, who developed the estimate, was familiar with cutting-edge developments in that area.

PROJECT AUDIT

The progress of the implementation of the project and the usefulness of the project deliverables are often evaluated using a formal project audit. A *project audit* is different from a financial audit in that it concentrates on all project attributes, a small portion of which includes the cost performance attributes. Ideally, the audit procedures for an outsourced project focus on the same indicators that are normally monitored during the progress-monitoring phase of an internal project. The project progress attributes to be audited should include those attributes that measure the pace of the project progress in terms of achieving the intermediate milestones, the cost of delivered items, and the quality or performance of the deliverables as compared with the most recent baseline. The audit may also take into account the behavior of contractor personnel, such as responsiveness and attitude.

By way of establishing a base of comparison, if the results of an audit deem an internal project no longer necessary or viable, that project can be terminated with reasonable ease. The personnel and equipment assigned to this internal project can then be dispersed throughout the organization somewhat systematically. However, unless the external project is being terminated due to the poor performance of the contractor in any of the triple constraint areas, terminating an external project is far more complex and costly.

If the contractor is progressing in a reasonably satisfactory pace at the time the project is terminated, then the client enters into a negotiation with the contractor to compensate the contractor for the cost of completed work, work in progress, mobilization for future tasks, early demobilization costs, and anticipated profits.

> If the project cannot be conveniently conducted within the organization, then an outside organization should be retained to implement the project. External projects add value to an organization quickly and without major administrative disturbance, although there is an ongoing debate regarding whether external projects are cost-effective, individually or as a concept. Additionally, some argue that external projects deflect any risks that might have had an impact on the funding organization, while others argue that external projects bring their own brand of risks to the organization, mostly related to finances.
>
> If the project has been clearly and carefully defined, then a fixed-price contract is appropriate. Otherwise, a service contract, usually known as a cost-plus-fee contract, is more appropriate. Independent of the mode of contracting, the client is often placed in a position of making tradeoff decisions. Therefore, the client should make every effort to monitor the progress of the project closely in order to be prepared to deal with consequences of unexpected project events.

NOTES

1. R. DeNeufville, and E. Hani, Bidding Models: Effects on Bidders' Risk Aversion, *ASCE Journal of Construction Division* 103, no. CO1(March 1977): 57-70.
2. M. Gates, Review of Existing and Advanced Construction Estimating Techniques, *Proceedings of 1978 Conference on Construction Estimating and Cost Control Methods* (New York: American Society of Civil Engineers Construction Division, July 1978), p. 31.

3. Anonymous, *A Guide to Project Management Body of Knowledge* (PMBOK®) (Sylva, NC: Project Management Institute, 2000).

4. Anonymous, *Parametric Estimating Handbook*, 2nd Ed. (Washington, DC: US Department of Defense, Spring 1999).

5. Anonymous, *Skills and Knowledge of Cost Engineering*, 4th Ed. (Morgantown, WV: AACE, September 1999).

6. M.R. Vigder and A.W. Kark, *Software Cost Estimation and Control* (Ottawa, Ontario, Canada: National Research Council of Canada, February 1994).

Bibliography

Anbari, F.T. *Quantitative Methods for Project Management* (New York: International Institute for Learning, 1997).

Anonymous. *A Guide to the Project Management Body of Knowledge (PMBOK®)* (Sylva, NC: Project Management Institute, 2000).

Anonymous. *Parametric Estimating Handbook*, 2nd Ed. (Washington, DC: US Department of Defense, Spring 1999).

Anonymous. *Richardson's Plant Cost Estimating Standards* (Mesa, AZ: Richardson Publishing, 1998).

Anonymous. *RS Means Construction Reference Books* (Kingston, MA: RS Means Company, 2000).

Anonymous. *Skills and Knowledge of Cost Engineering*, 4th Ed. (Morgantown, WV: AACE, September 1999).

Baker, J. Cost/Time Trade-Off Analysis for the Critical Path Method: A Derivation of the Network Flow Approach, *Journal of the Operational Research Society* 48, no. 12 (December 1997):1241-1244.

DeNeufville, R., and E. Hani. Bidding Models: Effects on Bidders' Risk Aversion, *ASCE Journal of Construction Division* 103, no. CO1 (March 1977): 57-70.

Foldes, S., and F. Soumis. PERT and Crashing Revisited: Mathematical Generalizations, *European Journal of Operational Research* 64, no. 2 (January 22, 1993): 286-294.

Gates, M. Bidding Model—A Monte Carlo Experiment, *ASCE, Journal of the Construction Division* 102, no. 4 (December 1976): 669-680.

Gates, M. Review of Existing and Advanced Construction Estimating Techniques, *Proceedings of 1978 Conference on Construction Estimating and Cost Control Methods* (New York: ASCE Construction Division, July 1978).

Gates, M., and A. Scarpa. Optimum Working Time, *ASCE Transportation Engineering Journal* 103, no. 49 (November 1977): 773-781.

Gates, M., and A. Scarpa. Reward-Risk Ratio, *ASCE, Journal of the Construction Division* 100, no. 4 (December 1974): 521-532.

Gould, F.E. *Managing the Construction Process: Estimating, Scheduling, and Project Control* (New York: John Wiley & Sons, 1996).

Ibbs, C.W., and Y.H. Kwak. *The Benefits of Project Management—Financial and Organizational Rewards to Corporations.* (Sylva, NC: PMI® Publications, 1997).

Jandy, G., and K. Tanczos. Network Scheduling Limited by Special Constraint As a Function of Time Cost, *Periodica Polytechnica Transportation Engineering* 15 no. 2, 1987.

Kerr, R.A. A System Fails at Mars, A Spacecraft Is Lost, *Science* 286 (November 19, 1999): 1457-1459.

Kerzner, H. *Project Management: A Systems Approach to Planning, Scheduling, and Controlling*, 6th Ed. (New York: John Wiley & Sons, 1998).

Kerzner, H. *Applied Project Management: Best Practices on Implementation* (New York: John Wiley & Sons, 2000).

Michaels, J.V., and W.P. Wood, *Design to Cost* (New York: John Wiley & Sons, 1989).

Navarrete, P. *Planning, Estimating, and Control of Chemical Construction Projects* (New York: Marcel Dekker, Inc., 1995).

Ostwald, P.F. *Engineering Cost Estimating*, 3rd. ed. (Englewood Cliffs, NJ: Prentice Hall, 1991).

Pulat, P., and S. Horn. Time-Resource Tradeoff Problem, *IEEE Transactions on Engineering Management* 43, no. 4 (November 1996): 411-416.

Rad, P.F. Deliverable-Oriented Work Breakdown Structure, *AACE Cost Engineering*, 40, no. 12 (December 1999): 35-39.

Remer, D.S., and C. Wong. Cost Scale UP Factors for Airport Construction, *Cost Engineering* 38, no.2 (February 1996): 24-26.

Schlick, H. Schedule and Resources of Fast Track Renovation Work, *ASCE, Journal of the Construction Division* 107, no. 4 (December 1981).

Sipos, A. Project Time-Cost Optimization with the Purchase Time Method, *Cost Engineering* 40, no. 7 (July 1998): 33-40.

Soumis, S., and F. Foldes. PERT and Crashing Revisited: Mathematical Generalizations, *European Journal of Operational Research* 64, no. 2 (January 1993): 286-294.

Stewart, R.D., R.M. Wyskida, and J.D. Johannes. *Cost Estimator's Reference Manual*, 2nd Ed. (New York: John Wiley & Sons, 1991).

Tahn, E., and E. Selcuk, Resource Constrained Project Scheduling Problem with Multiple Crashable, a Heuristic Procedure, *European Journal of Operational Research* 107, no. 2 (June 1998): 250-259.

Vigder, M.R., and A.W. Kark. *Software Cost Estimation and Control* (Ottawa, Ontario, Canada: National Research Council of Canada, February 1994).

Vrat, P., and C. Khenakrairut. Goal Programming Model for Project Crashing with Piecewise Linear Time-Cost Trade-Off, *Engineering Costs and Production Economics* 10, no. 2 (June 1986): 161-172.

Index

A

acceptance testing phase, 89
Actual Cost of Work Performed (ACWP), 78
allowance, 111
analogous estimates
    capacity factor, 54–55
    definition, 46, 53–54
    equipment factor, 54–55
    square root technique, 59–61
    three-quarters rule, 55–59
    two-thirds rule, 61–62
Association for the Advancement of Cost
    Engineering, 49
audit, 112–113
average internal rate of return, 8

B

BAC. *See* Budget at Completion
BCWP. *See* Budgeted Cost of Work
    Performed
BCWS. *See* Budgeted Cost of Work
    Scheduled
bids
    competition, 109
    contract price, 108
    estimates, 108
    profit margin, 109
bonus for underrun, 105
bottom-up estimate, 43
budget approval, 19
Budget at Completion (BAC), 78
budget preparation and approval, 69
Budgeted Cost of Work Performed (BCWP),
    78
Budgeted Cost of Work Scheduled (BCWS),
    78
buffers, schedule, 94

business case, 6
business plan, 6

C

cash flow constraints, 93
cash flow demand, 7
change, managing, 69
chief executive officer (CEO), 70
client reserve, 112
competitive necessity, 8
conceptual design, 22
conceptual documents, 24
concurrent engineering, 90
contingency, 112
contract process, 19
contracts
    administrative, 103
    bids, 103
    cost-plus, 104–105
    definition, 102–103
    fixed-price, 103
    lump-sum, 103–104
    technical, 103
    time-and-material, 104
    unit-price, 104–105
    winners, 103
cost
    estimating, 36–38
    schedule, relationship to, 2
cost-benefit ratio, 8
cost-duration relationship, 92
cost management
    change, categories of, 86
    change log, 84
    change management board, 83
    change request form, 83
    definition, 81

delivery schedule, 87
external projects, 83
feed-forward technique, 87–88
forecasting, 88
implementation phase, 85
performance variances, 82
purpose of, 85–86
schedule, impact of changes, 88–89
triple-constraint tradeoff decisions, 81
unexpected events, 82
CPM methodology, 70
crash point, 90
critical path activities, 90
customer education, 8

D

data capture forms, 70
data collection, 71
decommissioning, 94
deliverables, 90
delivery phase, 89
design, 23
design process, 19
desired delivery date, 4
detailed design phase, 23, 89
direct costs, 110
disposal costs, 94

E

early delivery, bonus for, 105
earned value
    example, 77–78
    monitoring progress, 75
    planning stage *versus* execution stage, 76
employee education, 8
estimates
    accuracy, 47–50
    analogous, 46, 53–54
    appropriation, 48
    bottom-up, 43
    capital cost, 48
    conceptual, 43, 48
    details, knowledge of, 44
    duration, 47
    early, 46
    environmental characteristics, 47
    expert judgment, 64
    feasibility, 48
    final, 48

level of effort, 45
manpower skill, 47
models, 46, 49
modular, 46
normalization, 64–65
operating systems, 47
order of magnitude, 43, 48
parametric, 46, 50–53
preliminary, 48
project objectives, 47
range estimating, 46, 62–64
ratio, 46
ratio estimating, 54–55
requirements, 47
resource availability, 47
risks, 44
scope, changing, 45
square root technique, 59–61
system complexity, 47
system size, 47
technology, 47
three-quarters rule, 55–59
two-thirds rule, 61–62
evaluation and approvals, 23
expert judgment, 64
external projects
    allowance, 111
    audit, 112–113
    bidding, 108–110
    client reserve, 112
    contingency, 112
    contracting, 99
    contracts, 102–105
    design specifications, 101
    direct costs, 110
    disadvantages, 99
    functional specifications, 101–102
    indirect costs, 110–111
    modifiers, contract, 105
    outsourcing, 99
    overhead, 111
    performance specifications, 101
    product specifications, 101
    scope creep, 102
    specifications, 106–108
    specifications, importance of, 100

F

failed projects, 5

fast tracking, 90
feasibility, 8
feed-forward technique, cost management, 87–88
forecasting, 88

G

guaranteed minimum, 105

H

hardware, 19
high-level support, 8
historical data, 69

I

implementation costs, 95
implementation phase, 2, 89
indirect costs, 110–111
information retention, 8
initial cost estimates, 1
innovation, 8
integration, 19, 89
internal recognition, 8

L

late delivery, penalty for, 105
lifecycle costs, 94–95

M

marketing considerations, 8
modifiers, contract, 105

N

net present value, 8
normalization, 64–65

O

objective statement, 4
objectives, organizational, 5–6
OBS. *See* organizational breakdown structure
old equipment, removal of, 23
on-budget probability, 8
on-time probability, 8
100 point project scoring system, 9–10
operational necessity, 8
optimum duration, 93
organizational breakdown structure (OBS), 11
organizational objectives, 5–6

organizational priorities, 19–21
organizational support, 8
outsourcing, 35
overhead, 111
overlapping *versus* serial project stages, 91
overrun cost sharing, 105

P

parametric estimating
    modular model, 50
    parametric model, 51–53
payback period, 8
penalty for overrun, 105
PERT methodology, 70
PMO. *See* project management office
preliminary design phase, 89
procurement specifications, 23
product line extension, 8
productivity
    change, 79
    client factors, 79
    learning curve, 79–80
    measurements, 78
    project team, 78–79
profit margin, 109
profitability, 8
progress monitoring
    data collection, 71, 73
    definition, 67
    deliverables, 74
    earned value, 75–78
    effort, 74
    impact, 68
    indicators, 74
    organizational commitment, 69
    plan, developing, 70–73
    productivity, 78–80
    project management office, 68–69
    start date, 74
    work days, 74
progress reporting, 69
progress reports, 72
project audit, 112–113
project closeout, 19, 23
project compression, 92
project management
    importance of, 19
    operational tools, 70
    principles, 69

procedures, 69
Project Management Institute, 49, 78
project management office (PMO), 68–69
project mobilization, 69
project monitoring, 19
project objectives, defining, 3
project selection
    average internal rate of return, 8
    cash flow demand, 7
    considerations, 6
    cost-benefit ratio, 8
    models, 7
    net present value, 8
    payback period, 8
    ranking, 7
    total cost, 7
project stages, 89
prototype development phase, 89
public recognition, 8
purchasing, 19

Q

qualitative indices, 8

R

range estimating
    definition, 46, 62
    elemental values, 63
    PERT technique, 62–63
    probabilistic elemental costs, 63
rapid application development, 90
RBS. *See* resource breakdown structure
reduced fee, 105
reporting, 19
requirement analysis phase, 89
requirement statement phase, 89
requirements specifications, 2–3
resource breakdown structure (RBS)
    cost, 29, 36–38
    credential discipline basis, 36
    developing, 31
    each, 28
    effort, 28
    estimates, 28–29
    example, 29–30, 38–42
    fees, 32–33
    installed equipment, 32–33
    labor, 32

licenses, 32–33
machinery, 32–33
mapping WBS into, 34
materials, 32
money, 33–34
outsourcing, 35
people, 32, 35–36
position title basis, 36
primary division basis, 32–34
rate, 28
resource intensity, 28
resources, 27
tools, 32–33
work breakdown structure, relationship to, 11–12
work function basis, 36
resource requirements, 23
risk
    assessments, 95
    contingency funds, 96–97
    expenses, 96
    management, 96

S

schedule, 2, 69
scope, 2–3, 69
serial *versus* overlapping project stages, 91
software, 19
software development projects, 93–94
specifications
    cost-plus contracts, 106
    fixed-price contracts, 106
    responding to, 107–108
    scope, 107
system design phase, 89
system documents, 19
system requirements, 23
system testing phase, 89
systems engineering, 19

T

team attributes, 4
total cost, 7
turnover phase, 89

U

underrun, 105
unit testing phase, 89
user support, 19, 20

V

value analysis, 94
value engineering, 19
value to customer, 8
value to shareholders, 8

W

work breakdown structure (WBS)
  administrative unit basis, 14, 16
  ambiguity, avoiding, 21–22
  budget account basis, 14
  budgeting, 12
  case example, 15–16
  cost estimates, 12
  definition of work, 12
  deliverable-oriented base, 13, 17–19,
    22–25
  developing, 13

  expenditures, 12
  functional basis, 14, 17
  importance of, 1–2
  levels, 13
  performance, 12
  physical area basis, 14, 17
  process-oriented projects, 17–19
  product basis, 14, 17
  productivity, 12
  project plan, changes to, 12
  resource allocation, 12
  resource-oriented base, 14
  schedule-oriented base, 14, 16, 22–25
  scheduling, 12
  sequential basis, 14
  task activity basis, 14
  time estimates, 12
workload demand, 8